Stephen M. Vail

The Bible Against Slavery

Stephen M. Vail

The Bible Against Slavery

ISBN/EAN: 9783744731263

Printed in Europe, USA, Canada, Australia, Japan

Cover: Foto ©Lupo / pixelio.de

More available books at **www.hansebooks.com**

THE

BIBLE AGAINST SLAVERY,

WITH

REPLIES TO THE "BIBLE VIEW OF SLAVERY," BY
JOHN H. HOPKINS, D. D., BISHOP OF THE DIOCESE
OF VERMONT; AND TO "A NORTHERN PRES-
BYTER'S SECOND LETTER TO MINISTERS
OF THE GOSPEL," BY NATHAN LORD,
D. D., LATE PRESIDENT OF DART-
MOUTH COLLEGE; AND TO
" X," OF THE NEW-HAMP-
SHIRE PATRIOT.

By STEPHEN M. VAIL, D. D.,

Professor of Biblical and Oriental Literature in the Methodist General Biblical Institute, Concord, N. H.

" CONTROVERSY IS THE WIND BY WHICH THE TRUTH IS WINNOWED."—*Lord Bacon.*

CONCORD:
FOGG, HADLEY & CO., PRINTERS.
1864.

PROF. STEPHEN M. VAIL, D. D.

Dear Sir:—We the Students of the Methodist General Biblical Institute, having learned that the New Hampshire Patriot has closed its columns against you not allowing you to reply to the late pro-slavery articles of Mr. X., and believing that the Institution of Slavery is at War with the Bible and the best interests of our Country and Humanity, and believing that the publication of your reply to X and others at this time would be useful to the religious community and the Country generally, showing as we understand you do, that the Bible is against Slavery ; we respectfully solicit from you your reply for publication.

With Respect,

Your Obedient Pupils,

J. HENRY OWENS, ⎫
J. T. HAND, ⎬ Committee.
THEO. L. FLOOD, ⎭

CONCORD, Feb. 15, 1861.

To Revs. J. HENRY OWENS, ⎫ Committee of Students
       J. T. HAND, ⎬ of
       THEO. L. FLOOD. ⎭ Biblical Institute.

Dear Brethren :—Wrong or dishonorable action always fails, in the long run, to compass its ends. If the New Hampshire Patriot had given me as much space as my opponent X. occupied in its columns, this proposed pamphlet would not have seen the light. The Patriot's refusal to allow me to reply in the way desired, renders it necessary for me to reply in some other form. The form of the pamphlet will be more permanent and will in the end reach a larger circle of readers. Thanking you for your kindness, I cheerfully submit my manuscript to you for publication, as you request.

Your affectionate Friend and Teacher,

STEPHEN M. VAIL.

THE BIBLE AGAINST SLAVERY.

PREFATORY.

The question whether the Bible is against Slavery is at this time one of the highest interest. In the providence of God the people of the United States are now called upon to decide on the question of the permanent emancipation of four millions of slaves. Until the present rebellion got up and sustained altogether by the slaveholders and their abettors in the southern States, the people were united in the view that the General Government had no power of a political kind over slavery in the States. But now as the seceded States have taken themselves from under the protection of the Constitution and Government of the United States, and have rebelled against the government of the country for the sake of the better preserving slavery, their institution is no longer entitled to the protection of the government. And as a war measure therefore, and as a measure of justice, the slaves in the seceded and rebel States, with some exceptions, were declared to be free men on the 1st of January, 1863, by the President and Commander-in-Chief of the Army and Navy of the United States.

But many of our fellow citizens still claim that the Proclamation is only a war measure, and that its power must cease on the re-construction of the Union, and that the slaves must fall again into their former status.

The question of course must be settled by the people themselves of the whole country. If the President and Congress to be chosen in 1864, the present year, should be pro-slavery then all the acts of Mr. Lincoln's administration so far as the slaves are concerned might be abrogated, and

slavery for the slaveholding States so called would still be
the policy of the Nation. The great question before the nation in the coming presidential election must therefore be
slavery or no slavery?

As a christian nation receiving the Holy Scriptures as our
guide, it becomes a grave inquiry *what saith the Scriptures* on
this question? If the Bible is against slavery it is important to know it. If the Bible be found, after all the efforts
of slavery, to be on the side of Freedom it will be a confirmation of its Divinity to the minds of millions, and the Bible
will be dearer than ever to the hearts of all mankind. If as
many have claimed, it be against human liberty and in favor
of oppression, the inference will continue to be drawn by
thousands that it is not from heaven. My own belief is that
it has been greatly misunderstood,—and such has been the
traditional power of slavery over us, that as yet we have
only faintly apprehended the truth,—that the Bible is always
and every where against slavery.

§ 1. *Introduction.*

My object in the present publication is to show that the
Scriptures are against slavery, both those of the old Testament and of the New, both alike condemn it. By consequence
I must show that the recent publications of such writers as
Bishop Hopkins, of Vermont, Dr. Lord late President of
Dartmouth College, " X " of the New Hampshire Patriot and
others, who have written on the pro-slavery side of the question, are on a sandy foundation without the slightest support
from the Holy Scriptures.

It is not surprising that a system of iniquity of such pecu-
niary and political power as slavery in our country, should
find apologists among respectable men, and even among men
of reputed learning. But it is a matter of surprise at this
late day when this accursed system has put its cruel hand to
the throat of the nation and seeks the destruction of the Re-
public, and when all loyal slaveholders themselves are seek-

ing the destruction of slavery, that such men as Bishop Hopkins and Dr. Lord yet apologise for it and seek to save it.

But it must go down. The nation must and will slough off the horrid excrescence. There is no decree in the book of fate more certain than that *slavery must now be destroyed.*

Having long been of the opinion that there was no support for it in the sacred writings, the Holy Scriptures, I here present a candid review to the country of those passages which have been supposed by the gentlemen named above, and by others, as favoring involuntary servitude among men.

In the fall of 1862, soon after the issue of the President's Proclamation, that on the first of January, 1863, he should declare the slaves of rebels free on the ground of military necessity, the young men of the Biblical Institute invited me to preach on the occasion of said proclamation. The sermon was published. It was attacked in the New Hampshire Patriot. I replied to the attack, and challenged my reviewer to find a single case of justified sale of a human being in the Scriptures. It was replied that if there were no cases of such sale, that there were laws regulating such sales, and an attempt was made to produce them, to which I replied, and my reviewer then goes on to discuss the subject generally in opposition to my reply.

He having occupied some fourteen columns in the Patriot in opposition, while I had occupied but seven, I sought the privilege of further reply and was denied, at least till after the March elections. I am thus compelled to resort to this mode of self-vindication, as well as the vindication of the truth.

I would remark further by way of introduction, that I have kept the original Scriptures constantly before me, in all my discussions. Knowing that this must be the ultimate standard of appeal, I have sought to draw light from the Scriptures alone. And thus purposely while writing this reply I have not consulted other writers on the anti-slavery side of the question; but have constantly appealed to the Scriptures themselves. Comparing dark passages with their parallels, thus comparing Scripture with Scripture, and leaving all to be decided by the common sense of my readers. It has been gratifying to me to find, after my reply was written, that there is a substantial agreement between myself and such writers as Albert Barnes, Charles Elliott, D. D., and G. B. Cheever, D. D. The works of these writers are the most elaborate and most able of any that have fallen into my hands, and in my judgment they present, in general, the true scriptural views on this subject.

§ 2. *What is the meaning of the Hebrew gnebedh?*

[Pronounced differently by Hebrew scholars, some calling it *ebed*, others *gnebedh*, which I prefer.]

Other writers whose attention has not been specifically called to this subject have generally failed to discriminate between slavery and other kinds of servitude. So also the Lexicographers both of the Greek and Hebrew, e. g. Gesenius says *gnebedh* generally *a servant*, who among the Hebrews was also a *slave*. So Robinson, Lexicon of New Testament, *doulos, a bondman, slave, servant.* So others, all so far as I have observed, failing to properly discriminate between the signification *Servant* and *Slave.* From this looseness of defining as Dr. Cheever forcibly says, "The eggs of the Cockatrice are hatched." A Slave is an *involuntary, coerced servant,* held as property, a *chattel personal* in distinction from a *chattel material.*

A *servant* as distinguished from a *slave* is a voluntary servant, one who works for wages or a support. This confusion of the two words servant and slave, leads to much erroneous reasoning from Scripture. The condition of a servant is a normal condition, right, and often needful in human society. While the condition of a *slave* is always abnormal and wrong, and *never* necessary in human society, except as a punishment for crime. It is a condition born of pride, covetousness, and in a word, of man's evil nature. So St. Chrysostom says: " But if you ask whence slavery has its origin, and why it has entered into human life. * * * I will tell you; avarice, vulgar display, and insatiable cupidity begat slavery; since Noah had no slave, Abel had no slave, nor Seth, nor yet those after this." (Hom. in Epist. and Ephes. 22.)

The distinction between the two, *service* and *slavery*, *servant* and *slave* is clearly marked. The first is generic, the second is specific, the first is of labor in general, the second is of coerced labor. The first may include the second, and when so intended the sacred writers so qualify their language as to leave the reader in no doubt, as for example, when the children of Israel were called the servants of Pharaoh (*gnebedh Pargnoh*), we know slaves are meant, from the context. So Joseph was sold into Egypt for a *gnebedh*, *slave*, I should render, (Ps. 105: 17); for the account of Joseph's captivity shows, that he was a coerced servant, at least till he was raised to be Pharaoh's Prime Minister. So when Moses is called the *Servant of Jehovah* (*gnebedh Jehovah*), we must render *Servant of Jehovah* and not slave of Jehovah. So David is called the *servant of Saul* (*gnebedh Shaool*), not slave of Saul, for the context does not show that his service was coerced or involuntary. The distinction is perfectly plain, and the disregard of it by the pro-slavery writers mentioned above is very strange.

§ 3.   *What is the meaning of the Greek " doulos," and Latin "servus " ?*

We might as well say here, that the Latin *servus*, the Greek *doulos*, and the Hebrew *gnebedh*, correspond to the English word *servant*, and not to *slave*. Dr. Lord says, " An *ebed* at Jerusalem; a *doulos* at Athens; a *servus* at Rome; and a *slave* at Washington, have been as well understood, in those respective representative cities, to mean a chattel personal, as *son* has been understood to mean the child of his father.*

Dr. Lord, I respectfully submit, is not correct, although all the pro-slavery writers, as Bishop Hopkins, Fletcher, and others, agree with him. Let these gentlemen consider whether it would be proper to render Rom. 1: 1, Paul a *slave* of Jesus

---

* See second letter to ministers of the gospel, p. 48.

Christ, *doulos* in Greek, and *servus* in Vulgate, or whether it would be proper to render Is. 52: 13, (a beautiful prophecy of the Messiah), "Behold my *slave*," &c., Hebrew *gnebedh*, Vulgate *servus*, Sept. *pais*.

Observe further. The Lord Jesus Christ himself is called a *doulos* in Phil. 2: 7, "He took on him the form of a *doulos*." Does any one dare to say that He, who was found in the form of God took on himself the form of a *slave*,—an unwilling involuntary *slave?* Christ was indeed a willing servant to poor lost man. But he was not his unwilling slave, such an idea is not only absurd, it is impious. Yet to such a result the pro-slavery principle leads, and therefore is and must be *false.*

I say, then, that Dr. Lord and others are mistaken when they say that *gnebedh* is the specific term for *slave*. If so, then Moses was a slave, for he is repeatedly called *gnebedh*. See Deut. 34: 5, Josh. 1: 1, 13, 15, &c. Then Joshua was a *slave*, for he is also repeatedly called *gnebedh*, as Josh. 24: 29, Judges 2: 8, &c. Then also David was a slave, for he is called an *gnebedh* of Saul, 1 Sam. 30: 13.

Dr. Lord, and Bishop Hopkins, and "X," are simply mistaken in their declarations that *gnebedh* is properly a "*slave*." It is the general term for the English "*servant.*" It is generic, and includes all kinds of servants, and the specific sense must be determined by the context or connection;—e. g., when the children of Israel are called *gnebedh Pargnoh*, Ex. 9: 20, then it means *slaves* of Pharaoh; because the context shows that they were compelled to serve Pharaoh against their will, and without wages. When they are called *gnebedh Jehovah*, we are to render it *servants* of Jehovah, not slaves of Jehovah. So *gnebedheem David* is *servants* of David, not *slaves*, because these servants were clearly voluntary. I suppose the above illustrations will save me from being misunderstood.

I would further add that the proper word for *slave* in Greek is *andrapodon*, in Latin *Mancipium*. There is no word in Hebrew which specifically means *slave*.

Now for the interest we naturally feel in the opinions of others I would refer to Barnes on Slavery, p. 70, for his view of the meaning of the Hebrew *gnebedh*, which these writers so stoutly contend, always means slave. He says, "It is important to bear in remembrance that the use of the term *gnebedh, no where in the Scriptures of necessity implies slavery*."

Again, "for any thing that can be learned from the mere use of *the word guebedh*, the kind of servitude then existing [in the time of the patriarchs] may have had none of the essential elements of *slavery*."

Now turn to the work of Dr. Charles Elliott, of St. Louis, Mo., on the "Bible and Slavery" p. 33. He says: "The Hebrews used but one word—*ebed* or *abed*—to express all the relations of servitude of every sort, *abad*, the verb means *to labor, to work*. The noun *abed* derived from the last means a *laborer*, a *servant*. It is applied to a person who performs any kind of service."

"The Hebrews had two words to denote female servants, The one was *ama*, rendered maid servant, bond-maid, maid, bond-woman, maid, *etc*. The other was *Shiphcha* rendered *hand-maid, bond-maid, maiden, maid* servant. As far as the meaning of these words is concerned there is no countenance for slavery. Indeed, *the Hebrew language had no single word to denote a slave*, and the context, or peculiar phraseology, must be adduced to show that slavery or slave is intended, as no single word will answer this purpose," observe therefore that Albert Barnes and Charles Elliott, D. D., who have written the ablest books on the Bible and Slavery the age has produced, state the case in precisely the same terms that I have done.

§ 4. *View of the translators of the English version.*

It is a good cause of gratulation that our authorized English Version has in general taken the correct view of the Hebrew.

Bishop Hopkins, remarks that the word "slave" occurs but twice in the English Bible. But the Bishop is not quite correct. The word slave is found only once, Jer. 2: 14, "Is

Israel a Servant? Is he a home born [*Slave?*]" But here the original *gnebedh bayith*, does not necessarily imply a slave, and that the translators so understood this, is apparent from the fact that, they have italicised the word *slave* thereby showing that it does not belong to the original Hebrew.

The word "slaves" in the plural number is found only in the English Bible in Rev. 18: 13. "In this passage the votaries of Babylon or old Rome, the mother of Harlots, lament that no man buyeth their merchandize of gold and silver *

* and horses and chariots and *slaves* [greek *Somaton* of bodies,] and souls of men." Here doubtless slaves are meant and slavery is hereby branded as one of the abominable sins of the mother of Harlots, who makes merchandise of the "*bodies and souls of men.*"

Bishop Hopkins goes on to say that "the term servant commonly employed by our translators has the meaning of slave in the Hebrew and Greek originals as a general rule where it stands alone." The truth is precisely the reverse of this declaration.

The term "*servant*" commonly employed by our translators, *never* has the meaning of slave in the Hebrew and Greek originals when it stands alone, *i. e.* without being qualified by the context.

For example, the Israelites are called "Servants of the Egyptians," here it means slaves, because the context shows that their service was coerced or involuntary. So the case of Joseph. We know he was a slave, because the account given us in Genesis is that he was sold and used as an *involuntary* servant.

We inquire further: If the Hebrew original word, *gnebedh* —a man servant—standing alone, means a slave, why did our translators uniformly render it servant? This word occurs above 600 times in the Old Testament, and according to Bishop Hopkins, means "a *slave.*" Yet our venerable and learned translators have never rendered it "slave" in a single instance. This is certainly very remarkable, if the Bishop's doctrine be true. Then we have the term *amah*—a female servant—occurring also very frequently, but neither is this ever translated slave.

If now we turn to the New Testament, we find the original terms *doulos* and *doule*—man servant and maid servant—occurring more than one hundred times; yet they are never rendered slave by our translators in a single instance. I am only now calling attention to the fact that Bishop Hopkins has declared himself against the 47 translators of our English Bible. He has set up his authority against theirs on a question of translation. Now we have simply to say, that in our opinion Bishop Hopkins is in the wrong, and the translators are in the right. And we will proceed to vindicate the translators by an appeal to individual passages, and to the common sense of our readers.

Let the point be kept in mind. The Bishop says, "The term servant, commonly employed by our translators, has the meaning of slave in the Hebrew and Greek originals." We appeal to a passage claimed by the Bishop as sustaining his view, Gen. 9 : 25, "Cursed be Canaan, a servant of servants shall he be to his brethren."

The context shows that this is a prophecy of Noah in regard to his grandson Canaan. Inasmuch as he was never even a servant of his brethren personally, the reference must be to his posterity. Let us now read the passage with the amended translation of Bishop Hopkins. "Cursed be Canaan, a slave of slaves shall he be to his brethren." The Bishop, remarking on this passage, says, "The Almighty foreseeing this total degradation of the race, ordained them—the Canaanites—to servitude or slavery, under the descendants of of Shem and Japheth." But the Bishop did not observe that not only the Canaanites are slaves, but also that they are the slaves of *other slaves.* "A slave of slaves shall he be to his brethren." Our question then is, who are these other *slaves?* The Canaanites, the Bishop says, were slaves of the Hebrews. But to whom have the Hebrews been slaves? "All history," the Bishop says, "proves how accurately the prediction has been accomplished." The Hebrews as a nation were carried into captivity to Babylon, but not into slavery—and as a nation we are not aware that history reveals that they have ever been reduced to that condition. The Bishop must therefore review his translation, for the Jews never have been slaves, even according to his own definition, viz., "Slaves are servants for life, descending to their offspring."

History gives no evidence that the Jews have been slaves in this sense. They have been servants indeed in the sense that their nationality is dependent and has been dependent for many ages, and was dependent in the time of our Saviour, the nation then receiving Roman Governors, and paying tribute to the Romans. But they could not then be said properly to be slaves of the Romans. But they were, it is admitted on all hands *servants* to the Romans.

With this translation of the English version, the prophecy has been fulfilled. But we must deny that it has been fulfilled in the sense of Bishop Hopkins' rendering. We infer then that "servants" is the correct translation, and not " slaves."

Let any man take Cruden's Concordance and read under the word *servant* substituting the word slave therefor, and he will find himself led at once into the greatest absurdities: *e. g.* "Pharaoh made a feast unto all his *slaves*." The Lord will repent himself for his *slaves*. He will avenge the blood of his *slaves*. " Paul a *slave* of the Lord Jesus Christ, &c." It is into such absurdities that Bishop Hopkins leads his followers and readers. It is only needful to cite *one* example out of hundreds to refute his declaration, that the " term *servant* commonly employed by our translators has the meaning of slave in the Hebrew and Greek originals."

§ 5. *What is the meaning of the term "bond-man," in the English Bible?*

Our translators have rendered the Hebrew *gnebedh*, in about 20 instances "bondman." Thus the mere English reader gets the impression that slaves are meant, in such passages, in distinction from servants. But the original word is the same. And it is in my judgment a misfortune that this inconsistency appears in our English Version. Let the English reader then be upon his guard lest any inference from this fact be drawn unfavorable to free service, and favorable to the pro-slavery view.

I can conceive of no good reason for this variation from the common meaning—*servant*, unless it be in those cases in which *gnebedh* clearly refers to involuntary servants, as Deut. 6: 12, "Beware lest thou forget the Lord who brought thee out of the house of *bondmen*"—slavery or involuntary servitude in Egypt. See 6: 21, 7: 8, and others.

I have dwelt longer on this matter of translation, and the usage of the word *gnebedh* for the reason that here is the *proton pseudos, the beginning of error*, on the part of the pro-slavery writers. It does not refer to slavery at all, unless the context requires it, and never, I may say, when it stands alone.

§ 6. *What in a word, were the gnebedheem, servants, of the Hebrews ?*

In distinction from the *sakir* or *hired servant*, who wrought only by the day and lived with his own family, the *gnebedh* was attached to the family receiving his support and the support of his wife and children so long as he might wish to stay. Such servants were Eliezer in the family of Abraham, and Belhah and Zelpah in the family of Jacob.

See further remarks in following sections. The error of the pro-slavery writers is that they find no place for a class of servants between those hired and those enslaved.

§ 7. *Does the prophecy of Noah prove slavery ?*

The prophecy of Noah recorded in the ninth chapter of Genesis, seems to be regarded as the corner stone of the pro-slavery argument from the Bible. Hence all the writers under review elaborate it and refer to it again and again. Especially Dr. Lord and "X" of the N. H. Patriot. It is to them a precious "*douceur*"—a sweet morsel. But let them consider it attentively, and they will see that the hopes they have built upon this passage are entirely illusory. The prophecy with the context reads as follows:

Verse 20. And Noah began to be a husbandman, and he planted a Vineyard.

Verse 21. And he drank of the wine and was drunken; and he was uncovered within his tent.

Verse 22. And Ham the father of Canaan saw the nakedness of his father and told his two brethren without.

Verse 23. And Shem and Japheth took a garment and laid it upon both of their shoulders, and went backward and covered the nakedness of their father; and their faces were backward and they saw not their father's nakedness.

Verse 24. And Noah awoke from his wine, and knew what his younger son had done unto him.

Verse 25. And he said, cursed be Canaan, a servant of servants shall he be unto his brethren.

Verse 26. And he said, blessed be the Lord God of Shem; and Canaan shall be his servant.

Verse 27. God shall enlarge Japheth, and he shall dwell in the tents of Shem, and Canaan shall be his servant.

The reader will perceive that the point of the prophecy relied upon by the pro-slavery interpreters is contained in the 25th verse, " cursed be Canaan *a servant of servants shall he be to his brethren.*"

In order to make this apply to slavery they all with one consent give the passage another rendering. and quote *a slave of slaves* shall he be to his brethren. This being assumed without one word of proof, they are on the high road to the conclusion that slavery is divine. And that all the children of Ham, one third of the human family,—the people of Canaan, of Arabia, of Egypt, and indeed, of all Africa, are by the divine decree made slaves to Shem and Japheth forever. And these gentlemen seem to enjoy it as though they had really got into the pro-slavery paradise; and sit back in their easy chairs. and each says, "*I have servants* [*slaves*] *under me, and*

1 say to this slave go and he goeth, and to my other slave do this and he doeth it." A truly happy company!

And they are much better Christians than the anti-slavery white trash, the infidel abolitionists around them! They not only *know more* than others of the Christian family, but they are doing vastly more for Christ and his cause. " In a proportion of thousands to one!" says Bishop Hopkins. His words are, "*I believe that the number of negroes Christianized and civilized at the South, through the system of Slavery, exceeds the product of (English and American) Missionary labors in a proportion of thousands to one.*" The venerable Dr. Lord nods his assent to this bit of plantation logic, and little " X " of the New Hampshire Patriot becomes quite vociferous with the glorious idea of extending Messiah's kingdom by bringing its savage tribes under the dominion of slavery. I would suggest that he begin with the wild savage rioters of New York city, and the Pennsylvania coal mines! But we must return to Noah's prophecy. *Cursed be Canaan, a servant of servants shall he be to his brethren.*

What does it mean? Evidently that Canaan's descendants, in the far-seeing eye of Jehovah, should be brought down to the condition of servants to the descendants of Shem and Japheth. Canaan was the youngest son of Ham, Cush Misraim and Phut, being put before him. Evidently this curse is limited to the descendants of Canaan. But why should this prophecy be uttered at this time? The ill conduct of Ham had given the occasion, and hence it was proper that it should now be spoken. So far as the account goes, Ham's conduct was only slightly criminal. It was not because of Ham's conduct, nor on account of anything that Canaan had done that this malediction was pronounced; but simply as a prophecy as to what would be the history of the descendants of Canaan. The tenth chapter of Genesis, the 15th, 16th, 17th, 18th and 19th verses, shows who the descendants of Canaan were, and where they settled.

Verse 15. And Canaan begat Sidon his first born and Heth,

Verse 16. And the Jebusite, and the Amorite, and the Girgasite,

Verse 17. And the Hivite, and the Arkite, and the Sinite,

Verse 18. And the Arvadite, and the Zemarite, and the Hamathite; and afterward were the families of the Canaanites spread abroad.

How far they were spread appears from the next verse.

Verse 19. And the border of the Canaanites was from Sidon, as thou comest to Gerar, unto Gaza; as thou goest unto Sodom, and Gomorrah, and Admah, and Zeboim, even unto Lasha.

From these sons of Canaan sprang the seven nations of Canaan, who were subdued by Joshua, as we learn from Joshua 12: 7, 8.

Verse 7. And these are the kings of the country which Joshua and the children of Israel smote on this side Jordan on the west, * * * which Joshua gave to the tribes of Israel for a possession.

Verse 8. * * * The Hittites, the Amorites, and the Canaanites, the Perizzites, the Hivites, and the Jebusites.

These and these alone were the people referred to in the curse, " cursed be Canaan." It had no reference whatever to the other families of the children of Ham.

Every one will see who is at all acquainted with Biblical history, how wonderfully this prophecy has been fulfilled in the case of the Canaanites. Subdued by Joshua, they have never gained their independence to this day.

First, they became subject to the Jews, then to the Babylonians, then the Persians, Greeks and Romans, and for many ages have been subject to the Turks, and are such at the present hour. They are described by Dr. Robinson as existing at the present day, in the valley of Jordan, and in the low lands along the Mediterranean, in the Plains of Sharon. A poor despised people, servants of the Arab tribes who are at the same time under the Turkish yoke,* and it may be said that

---

* The Canaanites were a distinct people and servants to the Jews in the time of Solomon. See 1 K. 9: 20-22.

In Matt. 15 : 22, 59, we have an affecting account of a Canaanite woman

the Turks are servants or dependents on the Western Powers, France and England, and have been for nearly half a century. Thus it is that Canaan is a *servant of servants*, and Japhet is enlarged and dwells in the tents of Shem.

Thus it is that the prophecy is strangely fulfilled in the descendants of Canaan.

Now we could prove negatively that Ham's other sons have not been and are not subject in this sense to any other people. Misraim settled in Egypt, Phut in Morocco, and Cush in Ethiopia. Egypt, under various dynasties has generally maintained her independence of all foreign powers. And the Negro tribes of Northern, Central and Eastern Africa have also been generally independent, and in no proper sense could be said to have been "servants to Shem and Japheth." The prophecy is fulfilled alone in a non-negro race, the Canaanites of Palestine, and by no other, and has nothing to do with the people of Africa, or the other descendents of Ham.

The Canaanites were servants after the conquest of Joshua. They continued to be servants till the time of our Lord, in the sense of being a subjugated people. They are servants at the present day—voluntary servants, to the people among whom they dwell; but I have not yet been able to learn that they have ever been *enslaved*. They are servants in the sense that the Irish people are servants of the English Crown; but the Irish people are not slaves, nor have the Canaanites ever been slaves, so far as I can learn, in any period of their history. And yet Dr. Lord, Bishop Hopkins, and "X," all unite in the opinion that they were slaves, and not only they but the entire family of Ham was under the curse pronounced only upon Canaan, and that all alike were destined to slavery. But in each case the proof is wanting. They give us lordly assertion enough, but an infinitesimal amount of proof. *e. g.* Dr. Lord says, p. 53:

whose daughter was possessed of a devil, and who came to our Lord and earnestly besought him to have mercy on her. This incident shows that the Canaanites were still a distinct people in the time of our Saviour, but let us observe that there is no evidence that she was a slave.

2

" The offended sire looked only upon the son who had dishonored him."

And how Dr., had poor Ham dishonored his father? He happened to open his eyes and see him in his disgraceful plight of drunkenness and nakedness, and turned away as any pure minded man would, and yet you add he was " *Cainish*," of *Cainish* propensities, of *Cainish* associations, and his influence was *Cainish*. And the conclusion is that all of poor Ham's posterity must therefore be doomed to slavery. All this reasoning and poetry lacks only one thing, and that is *terra firma* on which to rest.

Furthermore, Dr. Lord will have it that there is a connection between *Cain* and *Canaan*. There is indeed a slight likeness in the sound of the two words, but no connection at all in the etymology or in the meaning. The two men lived two thousand years apart. This is all the connection there is between them! Cain slew his brother, but Canaan committed no crime, so far as the scriptures tell us. His descendants became corrupt and wicked, and thus in the just judgments of God were subject to Israel, but this was not till centuries after the father was in his grave. But the " Histories relate [what histories?] that the exterminated Canaanites fled in all directions to the wilds of Africa, as evidence is not wanting with their *Cainish mark* [a black skin] upon them." The venerable and learned doctor could not possibly leave out this old wives fable, from his second letter. His reference is to Gen. 4:15. God gave a *sign—oth—to Cain*, &c., not put a *mark* [a black complexion] upon him. For this there is no authority in the usage of the word.— Please, Doctor, look at your Hebrew Bible!

But last of all " X" thinks he has found out the solution, the complete demonstration that slavery is divine, from the *prophecy of Noah*.

And what is this demonstration? It is briefly as follows: That Noah's prophecy indicated the *divine* will,—that the divine will is right ;—therefore *slavery is right, and divine.* But is Mr. X, sure that prophecy always indicates the divine will, and that whatever is prophesied is always right?

Take the first prophecy recorded in the Bible, Gen. 3:15: " It shall bruise thy head and thou shalt bruise his heel."

Here the seed of the woman, viz: Christ is prophesied of as bruising the head of the serpent. Very well, this is according to the divine will, we say. But how about the other part? "And thou [serpent] shall bruise his [Christ's] heel." Is bruising Christ's heel according to the divine will? Is that right? You, Mr. X., or your principle, says yes! Then I say Judas Iscariot did right when he betrayed the Lord, for that was prophesied. Then the devil did right when he entered into Judas, for that, also, was prophesied. Then, also, the Jews did right when they crucified Christ, for this, too, was prophesied. To such absurdities this principle leads you.

Take another case for illustration. The prophecy of the Lord to Abraham in Gen. 15:13: " And he said unto Abram know of a surety that thy seed shall be a stranger in a land that is not theirs, and shall serve them, and they shall afflict them 400 years."

Here is a prophecy that the children of Israel should be enslaved by the Egyptians, and greviously afflicted for hundreds of years, and for no fault of theirs. But according to this principle, that prophecy is God's declared will, this enslaving of Israel for 200 years and upward was all right! When God punished the Egyptians for doing his will, and that was of course all right. To such absurdities and contradictions this principle leads.

Need I present you another example? Take the prophecy of Jacob, recorded in the forty-ninth of Genesis. Jacob here prophecies some strange things in respect to his sons. He prophecies of Reuben, " unstable as water, thou shall not excel;" i. e. it was the will of God that poor Reuben should not excel! Of Dan he says, " He shall be a serpent by the way, an adder in the path, that biteth the horses heels." This, too, must be the will of God!—for it is prophecy. Of Judah he prophesies, "his eyes shall be red with wine." This, too, is the will of God. So slavery, drunkenness, robbery, are all according to the will of God, and all right! To such folly and wickedness the principle of "X." leads.

§ 8. *Was Abraham a Slaveholder?*

The passages relied upon by pro-slavery writers to prove that Abraham was a slave holder are Gen. 12:5, 16, and others which follow:

' And Abram took Sarai, his wife, and Lot his brother's son, and all their substance that they had gathered, *and all the souls that they had gotten in Haran*, and they went forth to go into the land of Canaan."

"And he [Abram] had sheep and oxen and he asses and *men servants* and *maid servants* and she asses and camels."

But I submit that there is no evidence in these passages that there were any slaves at all in Abraham's family. They only prove that Abraham had servants, voluntary servants, family servants, attached to him by ties of friendship, and it may be of consanguinity, they without the slightest coercion yielding their services and receiving in return the patriarch's fatherly support and protection.

The authority of Abraham may be compared to that of an Arabian Chief or Sheik, whose household is usually made up of voluntary dependents and their families aside from his own wife and children. It could not have been otherwise with a man in his circumstances. There were no laws in the Desert to restrain the runaway, and no fellow slaveholder to help him in case of insurrection. Besides, he was a wise, just and generous character, and could not seek to degrade and oppress his household. God testified of him, "*I know him*, that he will command his children and his household after him, and they shall keep the way of the Lord to do justice and judgment, that the Lord may bring upon Abraham that which he hath spoken of him." Gen. 18:19. There could not have been any of the oppressions of slavery, therefore, in the family of Abraham.

Job or Jobab was probably a cotemporary of Abraham, and whose possessions and servants were greater than those of Abraham. The spirit in which he exercised his authority as a master is seen in Job 31 : 13, and precludes the idea of slavery. We quote from the Hebrew;

> If I spurn my servant's or handmaid's right
> In their controversy with me ;
> Then what shall I do, when God ar'seth ?
> And when he visiteth, what shall I answer him ?
> Did not he who made him in the womb make him ?
> And has not *one* formed us in the womb ?

The next passage relied upon is found in Gen. 14 : 14, 15.

Verse 14. "And when Abram heard that his brother was taken captive he armed *his trained servants, born in his own house, three hundred and eighteen,* and pursued them to Dan."

Verse 15. "And he divided himself against them, he and his *servants,* by night, and smote them and pursued them unto Hobah, which is on the left hand of Damascus." [i. e. to the North of Damascus.]

The question is not whether Abraham had servants, but whether he had *slaves* or involuntary coerced servants, and whether these three hundred and eighteen trained servants who fought so bravely and so successfully for him were *slaves.* As a general rule slaves will not *fight for* their masters but *against* them, and hence the leaders in "the great rebellion," have not dared, after three years' fighting, and under the most powerful incentives, to put arms into the hands of their slaves. The slaves in such case would fight against their masters. The whole history of slavery has proved it. The circumstances mentioned then in this brief portion of Abraham's history is as good as demonstration that these servants were not slaves but his voluntary servants, honored and acknowledged by him as possessed of freedom and equal rights.

The next passage which comes in chronological order, and affects the question, whether Abraham was a slaveholder is Gen. 15 : 1, 2, 3.

"After these things the word of the Lord came unto Abram

in a vision saying, fear not Abram, I am thy shield and thy exceeding great reward."

"And Abram said, what wilt thou give me seeing I go childless and the steward of my house is this Eliezer of Damascus?"

And Abram said behold to me thou has given no seed; and, lo! one born in my house is my heir.

The question here is, *Was this Eliezer of Damascus a slave of Abraham?*

The fact that he was the steward of Abraham, and his heir in the event of Abraham's dying childless, seems to be at variance altogether, with the idea that Eliezer was an involuntary coerced servant or slave. "X" of the N. H. Patriot tries to avoid this conclusion by accepting the reading of the Septuagint as quoted by Dr. Adam Clark, "as curious." It reads as follows, *ho de whios Masek tes oikogenous mou houtos Damaskos Eliezer. The son of Masek, my maid servant is this Demascene Eliezer.*

Dr. Clark very well quotes it as a *curiosity,* which "X" in his simplicity takes for solid truth. But the sole authority for this variation from the Hebrew is the Septuagint, which in this case can be regarded of no consequence, inasmuch as the old Hebrew root *mashak* means *to possess,* and hence *meshek — possession,* and *ben meshek, son of possession* or *possessor,* hence the translation plainly should be *the possessor of my house [will be] this Demascene Eliezer.* In this view there is a universal agreement both among Jewish and Christian interpreters.— The Septuagint gloss is simply unnecessary and unauthorized. Besides it does not matter. If Eliezer was the son of a servant woman, it does not follow that he was a slave. And further the circumstances and position of this Eliezer clearly show that his service in the family of Abraham was not a coerced service. It was an honorable, dignified and responsible service, and was not likely therefore to be entrusted to a menial slave. Besides, how could he be an heir or a possessor of property and yet be a slave? How can a slave be an owner, who does not own himself? An essential idea of the word slave, is that he *belongs to,* or is the possession of another. Therefore a slave can own nothing, all that he is, and all that he has belongs to his master. Hence the idea of " X " is absurd and ridiculous that this man could be an heir of Abraham, and at the same time a slave; or the guardian of his son Isaac, and at the same time the slave of his son Isaac.

Eliezer was the steward of Abraham, all the property of the patriarch was put into his hands. He was the guardian of his son Isaac, as appears from Gen. 24: 1, 2, 3; we quote, "And Abraham was old and well stricken in age, and the Lord had blessed Abraham in all things."

2. " And Abraham said unto his eldest servant of his house [viz Eliezer] *that ruled over all that he had,* put, I pray thee, thy hand under my thigh."

3. " And I will make thee swear by the Lord, the God of heaven, and the God of the earth, that thou shalt not take a wife unto my son of the daughters of the Canaanites among whom I dwell."

Now let us look at the circumstances and see whether there is any good ground to believe that this man was a slave —a mere slave.

Abraham lived twenty years after this, (Gen- 25: 7,) and Isaac was forty years old, as appears from Gen. 25: 20, "and Isaac was forty years old when he took Rebekah to wife;" and yet this man Eliezer " ruled over all that Abraham had." He even had the guardianship of his son, went to Padan-aram, [Mesopotamia] and selected a wife for Isaac, made rich p: esents to the lady and the family of Bethuel, conducted the expedition back to Canaan, a distance of several hundred miles, through a desert country, presented the lady to Isaac and told him " all things that he had done," as a faithful steward and friend. If this man was a slave, he was treated very differently from what the slaves of the South are treated, and with a liberality and confidence unknown to slavery. I therefore infer that " X " has made a great mistake in claiming Eliezer to be a slave. There would at least be equal reason in claiming Queen Victoria's prime minister to be a slave.

A further question bearing on our inquiry *whether Abraham was a slaveholder* is the question as to the status of Hagar.— *Was she a slave?*

The account of Hagar and of her connection with the family of Abraham is contained in the 16th chapter of Genesis. From this chapter it appears that Sarah, Abraham's wife, had no children, and she had come to that advanced period in life which would preclude the expectation of children. Then the account says: Verse 3. *"And Sarai, Abram's wife, took Hagar her maid, the Egyptian, after Abram had dwelt ten years in the land of Canaan, and gave her to her husband Abram, to be his wife."* Abram took Hagar, and she was henceforth his wife. Verse 15. *And Hagar bare Abram a son, and Abram called his son's name which Hagar bare, Ishmael; and Abram was four-score and six years old when Hagar bear Ishmael to Abram."*

Hagar therefore was Abram's wife, acknowledged to be such by Sarah, accepted as such by Abram, and the mother of at least one of his children. Now let me ask, was she at the same time Abraham's slave? Could he sell her? or could he drive her from his house? or cease to provide for her as a moral man? or as a good man? This fact then sends this impious theory to the winds, that Hagar was his slave. A servant she had been, but now she is more, she is a wife. A secondary wife it is true, but yet a wife, and as such, having all the rights of a wife both legal and moral.

This consideration that she was Abraham's wife disposes of another very pious idea of Mr. "X". He says that the angel of the Lord, who was Jesus Christ, met her in the wilderness and told her to go back to her mistress and submit herself. Very well. But how submit herself? as a slave? Yes, says he, as a slave. Hence he makes the Lord Jesus a returner of a fugitive slave! He who said, "break every yoke, and let the oppressed go free," sends back to her bondage this poor panting fugitive! This is his version, and the absurdity as well as impiety of it is apparent.

I would observe further that this woman Hagar was a wife

of Abram, so recognized by the angel, subordinate indeed to Sarah, but yet a wife of Abram, and having her rights as such. The angel tells her to return and submit herself, and take her former place in Abram's family. She had her right to support and recognition as a wife to Abram, and it was best under the circumstances that she should so do. She did return, not as a slave, but as a wife, subordinate to Sarah, and for 15 years at least lived happily in this relation. Abraham loved Ishmael, and doubtless continued to love his mother. Thirteen years passed away, and the rite of circumcision was instituted. Abraham was now 99 years old, and Ishmael a lad of 13 years was circumcised, together with his father. About this time Isaac was promised, but Abraham, though he was glad that a son was about to be born to him, now a hundred years old, was yet full of solicitude for Ishmael. And Abraham said unto God, " O that Ishmael might live before thee. And God said Sarah thy wife shall bear thee a son indeed; and thou shalt call his name Isaac, and I will establish my covenant with him for an everlasting covenant, and with his seed after him."

" And as for Ishmael I have heard thee: Behold I have blessed him, and will make him fruitful, &c." Gen. 17: 18, 19, 20.

In process of time it is said Gen. 21: 9, " Sarah saw the son of Hagar the Egyptian, which she had born unto Abraham mocking, wherefore she said unto Abraham cast out this *amah* [*maid servant,*] and her son; for the son of this *amah* shall not be heir with my son, even with Isaac,—and the thing was *very grievous* in Abraham's sight because of his son, [Ishmael.]

Abraham was greatly grieved on account of this dispute between these members of his family, showing his tender regard for Hagar and Ishmael. But the Lord solved the difficulty as appears from the next verse, v. 12: " And God said unto Abraham, Let it not be grievous in thy sight because of the lad, [Ishmael] and because of thy *amah* [Hagar] in all that Sarah hath said unto thee, hearken unto her voice; for in Isaac shall thy seed be called."

Mr. " X" endeavors to press Gal. 4 : 22, into his service to show that Hagar was a slave, "For it is written that Abraham had two sons; the one by a bondmaid, and the other by a free woman." Paul's word rendered " bondmaid" is *paidiske*, but this is not the proper term for slave. If so, then Ruth the Moabitess was a slave, for she is called by this term in Ruth, 4 : 12, and that, after her marriage with Boaz. It means a *young woman* without any reference to slavery, we will quote, " Let thy house be like the house of Pharez, whom Tamar bear unto Judah, of the seed which the Lord shall give thee of this *young woman,—Paidiske*. I venture to say one cannot find a single instance, either in the Scriptures or in the classics where this word necessarily means a slave. The Greek grammarians say that this meaning *slave* is an improper meaning.* The argument therefore from Gal. 4 : 22, fails to show that Hagar was a slave. Nothing more is implied than that she was a maid servant in the family of Abraham.

Another argument supposed by the pro-slavery writers under review to prove Abraham a slaveholder, is the phrase " *bought with money.*" It is found in the law of circumcision Gen. 17 : 12, "And he that is eight days old shall be circumcised among you, every man child in your generations, he that is born in the house, or *bought with money of any stranger*, which is not of thy seed."

We observe that buying a servant does not imply enslavement. The purchase may be for the purpose of freedom, nor is that *property* always for which we have to pay. The pious Hebrew was required to purchase his first born, Num. 18 : 15, 16, 3 : 45, 51, Ex. 13 : 13, 34 : 20. He was moreover required to pay when he would release himself or his children from their vows. See Lev. 27 : 2, 8. It is probable that the heathen around Abraham held men as captives. The money paid by him may have been the ransom price for such.

We observe further, that it was an oriental custom to pay money to parents for their daughters when desired as wives.

---

*See Liddell & Scott's Greek Lexicon, and Phrynici Eclogae Nominum, Edidit C. A. Lobeck.

This was done in the case of Rebekah when Eliezer received
her for Isaac. Jacob wrought 14 years for his wives Rachal
and Leah. The beautiful Dinah was sought to be purchased
by Hamor, for his son Shechem, "Ask me never so much
dowry and gift, and I will give according as ye shall say unto
me; but give me the damsel to wife."—Gen. 34 : 12. So Boaz
bought Ruth. Ruth, 4 : 10. But no good man makes a slave of
his wife, *purchase therefore does not imply enslavement;* still
further, such purchase money may have gone to parents or
guardians for service, or it may be to the servants themselves. There is nothing in the context or circumstances to
forbid such a supposition.

But says Dr. Lord, If Abraham purchased, then somebody
must have sold. Very true! But the appropriate question is
not whether the vicious heathen sold, but rather whether
Abraham himself sold? and whether such selling was justified by the Lord? If slavery is a divine institution selling
men would be equally right and commendable with buying.
But further it is remarkable that we have no instances recorded of Abraham's selling. By the Mosaic law it is made a
capital crime. It is to be presumed therefore that the patriarchal period also disallowed it, inasmuch as the patriarchal
customs find their first written expressions in the Mosaic
law. It is equally remarkable that the Mosaic law while it
so explicitly forbids selling, says not a word against *buying.*
Hence all Christian people unite in their approval of buying
for merciful ends, or for the purpose of Freedom. The
United States have recently bought the slaves of the district
of Columbia. The English government paid the slaveholders of its West India possessions, 800,000 pounds as a ransom
for their slaves, and so other Christian governments, and
Christian individuals have done. But if the United States
should sell men, as cattle in the market the act would be ex-
ecrated by the whole christian world. As we hear nothing
of slave sales, or of slave pens, or of slave chains, or manacles in the history of the patriarchs, it is fair to conclude
that there was no slavery among them.

It is pertinent further to ask, if Abraham did hold slaves, and buy and sell, would that prove its rightfulness? Abraham had more than one wife, is Polygamy therefore right? He deceived the King of Egypt; is deception therefore right? So that however the question be viewed, slavery fails of confirmation and proof.

Another passage appealed to by pro-slavery writers and especially by X., is the law of circumcision recorded in Gen. 17: 12, and reads as follows: " And he that is eight days old shall be circumcised among you, every man child in your generations, he that is born in the house, or bought with money of any stranger, which is not of thy seed."

The phrases relied upon to infer slavery are *he that is born in the house, or bought with money.* As to the phrase "bought with money" we need say nothing further, than what has just been said above.

The phrase "*he that is born in the house,*" implies doubtless the children of oriental servants in distinction from the children of the master, but herein is no implication of slaves; as voluntary servants bear children as well as those that are involuntary!

We go even further and say that the internal evidence afforded by the passage is positively against slavery. Here is a solemn command of the Almighty upon Abraham to circumcise all the various classes of male children connected with his extensive house-hold. He must not pass by any—all must be brought into covenant relation, and brought into the church and be made members of the same by this solemn rite.

In circumcision, it was implied that the child was given to God, to serve and honor God, as long as he might live. He must keep God's Sabbaths, he must not commit adultery. He must provide for his own father and mother, and wife and children. How inconsistent all this is with slavery! How can a slave have a wife? When his wife is at the control of her master? How can a slave train up his children, when those children are the property of another? How can a slave keep the Sabbath, when all his time and talents and blood and muscle and soul belong to another man? What accursed mockery this whole business of circumcision must have been on the supposition that Abraham's servants were slaves! From the necessities of the case they must have been voluntary servants and not slaves.

Slavery is involuntary servitude, that is servitude against one's will. Indeed, it does not allow a slave to have any will. Thus it takes away the manhood of the slave, and hence it is a crime against nature and against God. Mr. X and Dr. Lord say it is a wrong when "abused," and forget that it is itself an abuse, from its inception to its wicked end. Through all its moods and tenses, always and everywhere it is against morality, and against religion. It is against morals in that it takes away the servants' rights to his wife, to his children, and to property, especially the avails of his own labor. It is against religion, cecause it takes away the servants' right to the free use of his conscience, and offerings and worship towards God.

There is another class of servants—*Family servants*, I would call them—found in almost every family of wealth and prominence, which Mr. "X" wholly ignores. A man of prominence, of intellectual or physical ability or wealth, attracts the weaker and more dependent around him. This is a necessity of human nature. The fact is common among all nations—heathen as well as Christian, and in all stages of society, from the savage to the most enlightened. The Arab Sheik, the Indian Chief, the English Lord, and the 5th avenue millionaire all alike must have their retinues of servants— not slaves. Some of them may be hired from day to day, but most of them are family servants and stay with him often for life.

Abraham was a man of wealth, distinguished for probity, and faith, and business, and as a leader in war. Hence he became a chief among the men of his time. He became a powerful Arabian Chief, and hence his servants (not slaves) were multiplied. Some of them were *bought with money*, redeemed from slavery, just as benevolent and wealthy men of the North used to purchase slaves escaped from the South. As money answers all things, so in this and other ways, Abraham obtained servants [not slaves]. I say not slaves, for it will be observed that while Abraham *bought*, it is nowhere said that Abraham *sold* his servants. Bu slavery implies the practice of sale.

In closing his remarks on the case of Abraham, Mr. " X " makes a number of inferences, one of which he states as follows:

"These transactions of this great period of the true worship in the olden time clearly indicate both *the right* and *the duty* of civilized Christian people to compel all similar classes of persons to abandon their heathenish ways of life, and to employ them in useful industry, and instruct them in the principles of the true religion."

In other words slavery is the great civilizer. Slavery is the great Christianizer. So Bishop Hopkins dares to say that slavery converts " *a thousand*," where the missionary societies of our time convert " *one !*" And Dr. Lord nods *his* assent! Slavery a christianizer withholding the word of God, and declaring it a crime to teach a slave to read! Slavery a christianizer, when out of three thousand colored soldiers enlisted in the lower counties of Maryland, not one was able to write his own name! Slavery a civilizer where out of thousands, no man has his own wife! and no woman has her own husband. The advancing armies of the Union have revealed the fact that most of the gospel these poor people have heard is, " *Slaves be obedient to your masters !*" Alas for our poor race if such are to be our Missionary institutions !

Plainly these gentlemen are in no sympathy with the great missionary efforts of the church of God. They have found a more royal road to civilization and religion and that is by the road of slavery !

§ 9. *Distinction observed between servants and property.*

" There is a clear distinction," a recent writer remarks,

" made between the servants of Abraham, and the things which constituted his property or wealth. Abraham was very rich, in cattle, in silver and in gold. Gen. 13: 2, 5. But when the patriarchs *power* or *greatness* is spoken of, then servants are spoken of as well as the objects which constituted his riches. Gen. 24: 34, 35. It is said of Isaac and the man waxed great, and went forward and grew, until he became *very great* for he had possession of flocks and possession of herds, and great store of *servants*, 26: 13, 14, 16, 26, 28, 29. When Hamor and Shechem speak to the Hivites of the riches of Jacob and his sons, they say, ' shall not their cattle and their substance and every beast of theirs be ours.' 34: 23. Jacob's wives say to him 'all the *riches* which God hath taken from our father, this is ours and our children's.' Then follows an inventory of property : ' all his cattle,' ' all his goods,' ' the cattle of his getting.' His numerous servants are not included with his property. Comp. 31: 43,—16, 18. When Jacob sent messengers to Esau, wishing to impress him with an idea of his state and sway, he bade them tell him not only of his RICHES, but of his *greatness*, and that he had oxen and asses and flocks and men-servants and maid-servants. 32: 4, 5. Yet in the present which he sent there were no servants, though he manifestly selected the most valuable kinds of property. 32: 14, 15. See also 34: 23, and 36: 6, 7.

In no single instance do we find that the patriarchs either *gave away*, or *sold* their servants, or purchased them of *third* persons. Abraham had servants *bought with money*. It has been assumed that they were bought of third parties, whereas there is no proof that this was the case. The probability is that they sold themselves for an equivalent; that is to say, they entered into voluntary engagements to serve him for a longer or shorter period of time in return for the money advanced them. It is a fallacy to suppose that whatever costs money *is* money or property." (Kitto's Cyclopaedia Art. Slave.)

§ 10. *Was Isaac a Slaveholder?*

Mr. X undertakes to show also that Isaac was a slaveholder from Gen. 26: 13, 14.

And the man [Isaac] waxed great, and went forward, and grew until he became very great.

For he had possession of flocks and possession of herds, and *great store of servants*, and the Philistines envied him.

Vagnabudda rabbah, much service. Sept. *georgia polla.* Margin—*much husbandry.* Vulgate, *familiae plurimum.* All this doubtless implies *many servants*, not as Mr. "X" says, "*a large family of slaves*," nor is it said that "Isaac received these people as a gift from his father," nor that "he held the children in the condition of their parents," nor that "he held them in perpetual servitude," all this is of Mr. X's imagination. These people were Isaac's dependants, servants, just as every oriental chief has his servants, and as every Laird or Lord of feudal times had his servants and dependants. There is not the first particle of evidence that they were slaves.— Where are the *whips*, the *drivers*, the *chains*, the *manacles*, the *slave auctions*, the *slave pens*, and the *blood hounds* of this oriental bondage? always the necessary accompaniments of slavery.

§ 11. *Was Jacob a Slaveholder?*

The evidence that Jacob was a slaveholder is likewise wanting. The fact that Jacob bought his wives, paying fourteen years of service for them was then, and is to this day, the common custom of the country. It does not show that the husband has the power to sell them or use them as slaves, nor is slavery proved to have existed in the family of Jacob by the fact that Laban gave to his daughter Leah, Zilpah his maid for a handmaid." 29: 24. So far as the history shows it was altogether voluntary in Zilpah to go with Leah, and the same may be said of Bilhah, v. 29, Rachel's maid. While it was entirely voluntary and pleasing and preferable on the part of these young maidens to go with the wives of Jacob, it cannot be called slavery. No whips, no driver, no coercion, is seen at all, in either of these cases. They were entirely voluntary, and the idea of slavery is therefore excluded. Need I tell you, Mr. X., that in the free States of our country, similar instances frequently occur. It is frequently the case even among us, that servants are not hired by the day or week or month. Persons often serve in families from their tender years, and are treated as members of the family, all wants are provided for, and the condition is usually preferable to that of the hired servant. But this is no slavery. I am astonished at the willful blindness of X., that he could not see this numerous class of servants. He has ignored them entirely as servants, making them all slaves.

It is proper to observe that Zilpah and Bilhah, at the request of Rachel and Leah, each became concubines or secondary wives of Jacob, and bare him children. This shows that they were not the low and menial people which slavery would imply.

Such is the evidence Mr. X. brings to show that there was slavery in the family of Jacob. It all falls short of the mark, and does not sustain his conclusions.

§ 12. *Did the Mosaic Laws ordain Slavery?*

This question must be settled by a direct appeal to these laws. And they are by no means so difficult and complicated and multitudinous as is commonly supposed. They are mostly found recorded in the 21st chapter of Exodus, commencing with the 2d verse:

Verse 2. "If thou get a Hebrew servant, six years he shall serve, and on the seventh year he shall go out free for nothing." If thou "get" a Hebrew servant, no matter how, whether by gift or by hiring for money, or on any other condition, you must not oblige him to work for you longer than the Sabbatic year; he shall then be free to leave. Is there any slavery or involuntary servitude in that I would ask? The translation of the English version, "buy an Hebrew servant," implies a seller. If the seller was any other person than the servant himself or his parent or guardian, this sale

3

would be unlawful and a crime, as appears from the sixteenth verse of this chapter. "He that steals a man, or sells him, or if he be found in his hand shall be put to death." So more fully Deut. 24: 7, "If a man be found stealing any of his brethren of the children of Israel, and maketh merchandize of him, or selleth him; then that thief shall die." If there is any selling in the case, therefore, it must be understood of the servant himself, or of his parent or guardian, and the service must be voluntary.

Verse 3. "If he came in by himself he shall go out by himself. If he be married his wife shall go out with him," i. e., if he came into service a single man, he goes out as such. If he came into service a married man, or if he marries a wife in the meantime, his wife goes out with him.

Verse 4. "If his master have given him a wife, and she have borne him sons and daughters; the wife and her children shall be her master's, but he shall go out by himself." If the wife owes service to the master, then she still remains to discharge that service though she must still continue as the servant's wife.

Verse 5. "But if the servant say I love my master, my wife and my children, I will not go out free;" then he has the privilege of staying, and his master must support him.

Verse 6. "Then his master shall bring him unto the Judges, (or unto God as the Hebrew reads,) to acquaint them with the fact of the servant's voluntary choice. "Then he shall bring him to the door or to the door-post and bore his ear through with an awl, and he shall serve him forever;" i. e. as long as he lives, or as long as his master lives, and as it is a case of voluntary servitude, he can stay with his master, without regard to the year of Jubilee. This case of voluntary service for life is one which frequently happens in almost every community; often a favorite servant is retained during life, the servant desiring it.

A father might sell his daughter as a maid servant, with the view of her becoming a wife, as appears from the seventh and eighth verses.

Verse 7. "And if a man sell his daughter to be a maid-servant, she shall not go out as the men-servants do," (on the Sabbatic year;) but shall remain still with her master, for the simple reason, as I apprehend, that she may have suitable opportunity to gain upon the affections and the interests of her master, so that he may be induced to make her his wife. This appears from the next verse.

Verse 8. "If she be evil in the eyes of her master, who has not fixed upon her for a wife, he shall let her go free, he shall not have power over her to sell her to a strange people seeing he hath dealt deceitfully with her," i. e. has failed to fulfil her expectations as to making her his wife. This idea that the father sells his daughter with the view of her becoming a wife is further confirmed by the ninth and tenth verses.

Verse 9. "But if his [the master's] son marry her, he [the master] shall do for her according to the custom of daughters," i. e., he shall do for her as though she were his own daughter; give her just the same dower.

Verse 10. "And if he [his son] take another woman, her food and raiment and her privilege as a wife he [his son] shall not diminish."

Thus the Mosaic law most carefully provides that a poor girl whose father has, by his poverty, been driven to sell her while she was yet a minor, and yet unmarriageable, should not be abused; her rights are most carefully guarded.

In Lev. 25:47, will be found the law in the case of the Is-raelite who became the servant of the stranger. The words are, "*If he sell himself* unto the stranger." Yet the 51st verse says that his servant was *bought*, and that the price of the purchase was paid to *himself.* This confirms our view presented in the comment on the second verse. In all the laws of this chapter there is not the slightest evidence of slav-ery. The servant sells his service, and puts the money into his own pocket; he has his wife and children and controls them. If the master is oppressive he can leave him, and dwell where he pleases. See Deut. 23: 15, 16. The master may keep him, yes, *must* keep him, till the Sabbatic year, and all his life, if he has a mind to stay. It is plain to see if there is any slavery here, the *master* is the greater slave!

Before leaving the subject, I would refer the reader to Exodus, 21st chapter 20th and 21st verses, which Bishop Hopkins takes as authorizing corporeal punishment, and hence he infers the lawfulness of slavery. Instead of the passage authorizing corporeal punishment and slavery, we should say it is rather a law against it. It reads as follows:

Verse 20. *If a man smite his servant or his maid with a rod, and he die under his hand he shall be surely punished* [with death according to the law, recorded in Gen. 9: 5, 6, not at the discretion of the judges as Bishop Hopkins]. Verse 21. " Notwithstanding if he shall continue a day or two he shall not be punished for he is his money," i. e.: The master might not be punished with death in this case because it might be presumed that the servant died from some other cause, and as a matter of fact whether punished by the judges or not, he is punished by the loss of service. In this sense it is that the servant is his money;—not that he has power to sell him for that would be a capital crime, Ex. 21:16, and Deut. 24:7, above quoted.

We would commend to Bishop Hopkins' attention the 24th and 25th verses commonly called the *lex talionis,* " eye for eye, tooth for tooth, hand for hand, foot for foot. Burning for burning, wound for wound, stripe for stripe." Can Bishop Hopkins say that this law was not for the servant as well as for the master? Is not the law rather for the protection of the poor and the defenceless, rather than for the rich and the powerful? If the law was executed literally then the servant and the helpless should have the benefit thereof. If the servant was maimed by his master then he must be maimed in return, and the servant moreover was at liberty to depart from his service, as appears from verses 26 and 27, of 21st chap. of Exodus.

§ 13. *Does the tenth Commandment prove Slavery?*

The tenth commandment is claimed by Bishop Hopkins,

and Mr. "X.," as clearly proving slavery. It reads as follows:

"*Thou shalt not covet thy neighbor's house; thou shalt not covet thy neighbor's wife, nor his man servant, nor his maid servant, nor his ox, nor his ass, nor anything that is thy neighbor's.*"

These gentlemen claim that the commandment recognizes *property rights* in men servants and maid servants. But if this be so then the commandment also recognizes "*property rights*" in a woman who is a wife. And if on this ground men servants and maid servants may be bought and sold at pleasure, then married women also may be bought and sold at pleasure. Mr. X., keeps himself entirely in the dark on this point, with what object I leave for my readers to imagine. But Bishop Hopkins has more logical honestly. He sees this difficulty and yields to its force, and acknowledges that a wife has a "right of property" in her husband. The true logical conclusion then is that the wife may sell her husband. But "neighbor's wife," implies the right of property in wives by husbands. Then *husbands* also may sell their wives. But if the possessive pronoun implies *rights of property*, then a man might sell his neighbor also. Thus Bishop Hopkins and "X.," get into a pretty mess of absurdities! An argument therefore which proves too much proves nothing.

But yet Bishop Hopkins goes with his logic and says that he is "aware that the wives of our days may take umbrage at the law which places them in the same sentence [condition rather,] with the slave, and even with the horse and the cattle. *But the truth is none the less certain.*" What think you of this logic wives and mothers of our land? which reduces *you* as well as the poor blacks to the condition of beasts?

§ 14. *Were the Canaanites enslaved by the Hebrews?*

The Canaanites or heathen in Palestine were the original possessors of the soil. God foreseeing their increasing wickedness promised the country to Abraham, but assured him it would be 400 years before they should come into possession, "for the iniquity of the Amorites is not yet full."

What right had the Jews to the land of Canaan? it has been asked. I answer they had no right except as God gave it to them. But God never acts without a good reason. He never punishes a nation as he punished the Canaanites without a good reason therefor. This reason is declared in several passages. The sins especially of licentiousness and idolatry, became so prevalent that God abhorred the land.

"Defile not yourselves in any of these thing," said he to the Hebrews, "for in all these the nations are defiled which I cast out before you. And the land is defiled, therefore I do visit the iniquity thereof upon it. And the land itself vomiteth out her inhabitants."—Lev. 18: 24, 25.

"All that do these things (viz: idolators, diviners, inchanters, witches, charmers, consulters with familiar spirits, necromancers,) are an abomination unto the Lord, and because of these abominations the Lord doth drive them [the Canaanites] out from before thee."

"Not for thy righteousness or the righteousness of thy heart dost thou go to possess their land, but for the wickedness of these nations the lord thy God doth drive them out from before thee."—Deut. 9: 5.

On this account, therefore, the Canaanites were dispossessed of their lands and became servants unto Isreal. Thus was fulfilled the prophecy of Noah, uttered more than a thousand years before: "Cursed be Canaan, a servant of servants shall he be to his brethren." This does not refer to the African race at all, but to the descendants of Canaan, the Canaanites who never went to Africa, and were the only descendants of Ham who remained in Asia. What now was the necessary condition of this people? Deprived of their landed possessions, they necessarily became servants to those who owned the soil. They must have bread to eat and raiment to put on. How could they get these things without giving their labor to the Hebrews? The Hebrews were not only the proprietors of the soil, but they must ever remain such. About twenty-five acres was given to each family, and it could not be alienated further than the year of Jubilee. The consequence was, therefore, that however prosperous a Canaanite might be in acquiring real estate, it would all revert to the Jewish owners on the year of Jubilee. It was his destiny then, and, indeed, of all foreigners, to be servants to the Hebrews and that forever, unless they left the country.

It must be borne in mind further, that this communication or declaration of God to the children of Israel was made while they were yet in the desert. God, as an anxious father, looks forward to the future and makes provision for his beloved children. He tells them of the land of Canaan, a land flowing with milk and honey. He admonishes them that when they get settled in that land they must treat one another like brethren. When it becomes necessary for a family to have a servant they should rather employ those of the Canaanites, than the children of their Hebrew brethren. That these Canaanites have become a low and miserable race by their vices, but yet they may be employed and had better be employed by you as servants than to be left as pests of society, without employment. They shall be in the land and in this relation shall be to you and to your sons " a possession forever," i. e., as long as you continue faithful to me, and continue to keep posession of the land. For God had already told them that if they fell into the vices of the Canaanites, they, too like the Canaanites, should be driven out of the land.

And we should observe further, lest oppressive service should be too uninterrupted, the Canaanite and heathen servants had their rest on each Sabbath day, and on each seventh or Sabbatic year, and on the year of jubilee received a full release and discharge, as the text plainly implies: " Proclaim liberty throughout all the land, to all the inhabitants thereof." We conclude, therefore, that there was no such thing as involuntary servitude, except for crime, under the Mosaic economy, among the Hebrews. After a careful review of the subject we must say, so far from slavery being an institution of the Old Testament, we find numerous denunciations of God against it, and its attendant sins, e. g. : " He that stealeth a man and selleth him, or if he be found in his hand he shall surely be put to death."—Ex. 21 : 16. "For they are my servants which I brought forth out of the land of Egypt. They shall not be sold."—Lev. 25 : 42. "If a man be found stealing any of his brethren of the children of Israel, and maketh merchandize of him, or selleth him, then that thief shall die, and thou shalt put evil away from among you."—Deut. 27 : 7. "Therefore, thus saith the Lord, ye have not hearkened unto me in proclaiming liberty, every one to his brother, and every man to his neighbor ; behold I proclaim a liberty for you, saith the Lord, to the sword, to the pestilence, and to the famine. Jer. 34: 17.

§ 15. *Does Lev.* 25 : 44, 45, 46, *prove the Enslavement of the Canaanites ?*

As this passage of Leviticus is the great proof text of pro-slavery writers we will examine it with special care. In order that the reader may the better appreciate our criticism we will offer together with the common versions, a literal translation from the original Hebrew.

English Version.

v. 44. Both thy bond-men, and thy bond-maids which thou shalt have, *shall be* of the heathen that are round about you, of them shall ye buy bond-men and bond-maids.

v. 45. Moreover of the children of the strangers that do sojourn among you; of them shall ye buy, and of your families that are with you which they begot in your land and they shall be your possession.

v. 46. And ye shall take them as an inheritance for your children after you to inherit them for a possession: They shall be your bond-men forever; but over your brethren the children of Israel ye shall not rule one over another with rigor.

Literal Version.

v. 44. Thy male servant, and thy female servant which shall be to thee from the heathen which are around about you—

from them ye shall get the male servant and the female servant.

v. 45. Also from the children of the transient people—the strangers with you, from them ye shall get servants, and from their families which are with you, which they have begotten in your land—they shall be to you for a possession.

v. 46. Ye shall inherit them for you and for your sons after you for a possession—always of them ye shall obtain service,—over your brethren the children of Israel—each man over his brother—thou shalt not rule over him with rigor.

The plain meaning of the law as here given by Moses is that his people should get their servants, as far as possible, first from the Canaanites, or heathen round about, and secondly from the strangers or transient people of the land, and not of their brethren the Hebrews, if it could be avoided. For the reason that each family of Israel might keep possession of its landed estate, and their children grow up in habits of industry, to the end that they might be a distinct and peculiar people, sending forth the light of the true religion into the midst of the surrounding idolatrous nations.

It will be seen that I have rendered the passage from the original Hebrew as exactly and literally as possible, and in *so doing it becomes divested strangely of its . proslavery shading. The words *gnebedh* and *amah*—"male servant" and "female servant," are plainly improperly rendered in our English version, " bond man " and " bond maid," inasmuch as it is against the usage, and the context does not require an extraordinary rendering. Besides, the English version in the above rendering is inconsistent with itself, as the very same words in v. 6, of this very chapter are rendered " man servant " and " maid."

These words with their cognates are used about one thousand times in the Hebrew scriptures, and are almost uniformly translated in our version " man servant " and " maid servant." If now we will turn to Cruden's Concordance, we will see that they are rendered " bond man " and " bond maid" in only a comparatively few instances, say about twenty times, and in these instances with no apparent good reason. Nothing, therefore, can be inferred in favor of slavery from the terms "bond man" and "bond maid," for the meaning of the original is simply male servant and female servant.

Neither can anything be inferred in favor of slavery from the term "buy"—"of them shall ye buy." The Hebrew *kanah* means to *obtain, acquire, get*. Now this *getting* servants may be by paying wages. The same root is used when Eve says in regard to young Cain, "*I have gotten* a man child from the Lord," she certainly does not mean that she had bought him of the Lord! (Gen. 4: 1.) So the wise man says, "Get wisdom, and with all thy getting, get understanding," [Prov. 4: 7,] not "buy" it; for wisdom and understanding are hardly articles of purchase and sale. So we see nothing can be inferred from this term in favor of slavery, or of buying or selling men, women or children.

It will be asked, perhaps, how I explain the words " inheritance " and " a possession forever." God, for example, is said to be the " inheritance " of his people. God is not therefore our slave! So again the Lord says to the son, in the second Psalm, "I will give thee the heathen for thy inheritance and the uttermost parts of the earth for thy possession."

The reader will observe that these words are not always used in the absolute and unlimited sense, so as to imply the power of sale and punishment. For example, a man holds in possession a wife or a child. Has he therefore the power of sale over them? or the right to whip and treat them as beasts of burden? It is said in the second Psalm that the heathen shall be given to Christ for his *inheritance*, and the uttermost parts of the earth for his *possession*. Is it therefore implied that Christ will make slaves of the heathen? The Hebrew words are the same in Leviticus as in the Psalms.

We speak of the British " possessions " in Asia—in North America—in the West Indies, &c., but do we mean to say, or to have any one infer that all the people or even any of them in the British Colonies are slaves?—no, not one. The people of India, the people of Nova Scotia, the people of New

Caladonia, and of the Island of Jamaica, &c., are all subjects or *servants* of the British Crown, but they are not slaves by any means. These countries are Queen Victoria's "inheritance" too, are they not? Has she not inherited them from her forefathers? Just so it was with the Canaanites. They were the *possession* and *inheritance* of Israel. They were subjugated by Israel. The Israelites took possession of their lands, and the Canaanites therefore became servants, tributaries, not necessarily *slaves*.

Great stress has been put upon the term "*forever.*" The reader will observe that I have rendered according to the Masonic accentriation, "*Always of them ye shall obtain service.*" This I prefer to the common version.

But if we adopt the rendering of the English version, the following remarks will be seen to be appropriate: The term "forever" must be limited according to the nature of the subject to which it is applied. The Jews for example were to have possession of the land of Canaan "forever." Not *forever* in its unlimited sense, certainly; but only so long as they might be obedient to God. As soon as they became rebellious and forsook the Lord, he suffered their enemies to drive them out. The hills are said to be "everlasting;" not literally, for they are gradually disintegrating, and the fires of the great day will melt them away. So we say in our conveyances of real estate; it is to be the grantee's *forever*—i. e., so long as he lives, or till he pleases to sell. The Canaanites were to continue in the condition so long as the Jews should hold the sovereignty of this beautiful land; but that has long since ceased, and the Canaanites are servants to the Jews no more. The Jews themselves afterwards became servants to the Babylonians, and then the Persians, and then the Greeks, and, finally, on their rebellion against the Romans, Josephus tells us that many of them were actually sold as slaves. So I venture to say it may be with the proud rebels of the Southern States; so soon as their lands are confiscated, they like the Canaanites, will become servants—not *slaves*—I hope.— But servants they are destined to become. It will, it must be so, if the just retributions of Heaven continue to men, as the just punishment for their crimes.

I would add before I close, that the critical views above presented are fully sustained by those venerable versions of the Hebrew Scriptures—the Septuagint,—the Vulgate,—and the Targum of Onkelos. Let the reader compare my translation of the above passage with theirs. They use no extraordinary terms as *bond-man*, &c. But the common *servus* and *ancilla*, *doulos* and *doula*.—And for "*buy*" *habeo* and *ktaomai*: no thought of *slaves* ever entered the minds of those venerable translators; they thought only of servants—servants employed, and servants paid their just and equal wages; or at least possessed of their liberty and a competent support, with the privileges of worship, of family and of marriage, as the law already referred to in Ex. 21: duly provided.

We have taken it for granted in the foregoing discussion, that the phrase " heathen which are round about you," refers especially to the Canaanites. Such was the location geographically of the children of Israel that the words "round about" in Lev. 25: 44, must refer to individual tribes or families, rather than to the nations. Palestine was bounded on the West by the Great Sea, on the North by the Mountains of Syria, and on the East and South by the Arabian Desert.— From the Syrians they could not get servants as they were powerful and independent peoples. Nor could they get them to any great extent from the desert tribes of Edom, Moab and Ammon. These people dwelling in the vast Arabian deserts were never subdued by the Jews for any great length of time. Nor were the Babylonians, Persians, or even the Greeks and Romans ever able to bring them into permanent subjection. This great and terrible desert, with very few fountains or wells of water, and these only known to those wandering nomadic, ancient Bedouin of the desert, has ever constituted an invincible barrier against invading armies.— And such has ever been the wild, warlike, independent roving habits of these desert peoples, that servants obtained from

them would naturally be of little worth. It seems necessary
therefore to refer the words " Heathen which are round about
you," to the Canaanites, perhaps exclusively. This is rendered further probable, by the law in respect to the Edomite
and the Egyptian as recorded in Deut. 23: 7.

"Thou shalt not abhor an Edomite, for he is thy brother.—
Thou shalt not abhor an Egyptian, because thou wast a stranger in his land."

It is therefore morally certain that the " heathen " referred
to are not the heathen external to Palestine, but the heathen
Canaanites in their midst.

Another fact that renders our view quite certain is the
mention of the transient people or sojourners or strangers, in
distinction from the Canaanites who were natives of the land.
Of these foreigners sojourning in the land, servants might be
obtained rather than of their brethren the Hebrews. Many
of these very likely were Moabites, Edomites, and also foreigners of other nations.

§ 16.   *What is the meaning of Lev. 22: 11 ?*

Let the reader bear in mind that slavery is involuntary
servitude; but all involuntary servitude is not slavery. There
is involuntary servitude for crime, as in the case of the thief.
The law is, " If he [the thief] have nothing, then he shall be
sold for his theft," (Ex. 22: 3,) or in other words, he must be
punished for a time by his giving his service to the party injured until proper restitution—five-fold, four-fold, three-fold
or two-fold be made. according to the articles stolen or the
amount of injury done. So we incarcerate for crime and subject persons to involuntary servitude, in our reform schools,
workhouses and State Prisons. But this is not slavery. ·

2. Our position is, then, that there was no slavery among
the Hebrews, and even that the Canaanite was no slave, inasmuch as his servitude was not compelled. The Almighty dis-
poser of nations had brought him into subjection to the Hebrews, had taken away from him his lands, but there is no evidence that He took away from him his personal liberty. He

had become very wicked, and hence was reduced to the condition of a servant, but not to the cruel condition of a slave.

3. Indeed, there is no word in the Hebrew which means specifically *slave, slavery* or *slaveholding*. It was needful to describe the thing, whenever there was occasion to refer to it. See the law recorded in Ex. 21: 16. "*He that stealeth a man and selleth him, or if he be found in his hand, he shall surely be put to death.*" Here is *enslavement*, "He that stealeth a man and selleth him." And then there is *slaveholding*, "if he be found in his hands." Both acts are alike capital crimes.

Lev. 22: 11, is supposed to involve slavery, by Mr. X, and reads as follows, in our version :—

" But if the priest buy any soul with his money, he shall eat of it, and he that is born in his house. They shall eat of his meat."

I would render the original as follows :—" *When a priest may come into possession of a person by means of his money, he* [the servant] *shall eat of it,* [i. e. the priest's food] *and one born in his house, they shall eat of his food.*"

I would paraphrase as follows; When a priest comes into possession of a servant, who is not hired, but is obtained by the payment of money to his parent or ward, such person becoming properly a member of the priest's family, is to be treated accordingly, and is to eat at the priest's table and of the food set apart for him; whereas a hired servant, who is hired for only a brief period, as a day or a week, is to board with his own family and not with the family of the priest.— So likewise every child born in a priest's family, whether it be a child of his own or a child of his son, such child is to be provided for and is to be considered a legitimate member of his family, and has a right to support out of the priest's stipends.

The passage therefore does not prove slavery. The fact of purchase does not imply enslavement. We often purchase in order to set free; and among the orientals it was and still is common to purchase wives, and parents and wards often sell their girls with the view of their becoming wives. For ex-

ample, Jacob paid his father-in-law, Laban, fourteen years of
faithful labor for his two wives, Sarah and Rachel, (Gen. 29):
but this does not imply that Jacob made slaves of his wives.
So Hamor wished to purchase Dinah, the beautiful daughter
of Jacob, for his son Shechem, not for the purpose of making
her his slave, but the honored wife of his son. (See Gen.
34: 8, and following verses). So the prophet Hosea purchased him a wife for fifteen pieces of silver and one and a
half homers of barley. (Hos. 3: 2). That this was a common practice appears further from Ex. 22: 17. 1 Sam. 18:
25. Wives are thus purchased in the East at the present
day. (See Harmer's observations, vol. 2, p. 513.)

Then there was another class of persons obtained by money,
who became more than hired servants—even proper members
of the family. They were usually young persons from poor
families, whose parents often found it for their advantage to
sell the services of their children during their minority, i. e.,
till twenty years of age. So persons might sell themselves
until the Sabbatic year as permanent servants. Thus their
condition became usually preferable to that of a hired servant, which changed with every varying season or cloudy day.
These classes of servants and the rules respecting them, are
laid down in the twenty-first chapter of Exodus. See verses
7, 8, 9, 10, especially, and comments on, section 12.

Thus the Mosaic law most carefully provides that a poor
girl, whose father has by his poverty been driven to sell her
while yet a minor, and yet unmarriageable, should not be
abused. Her rights are most carefully guarded. How different this is from slavery! I need not stop to point it out.
Now was it not fit that this class of persons should sit at the
priest's table as one of his own children, and eat of the con-
secrated food, which was called *kodesh* or *holy?* This law,
therefore, so far from implying *slavery*, was a kind and merciful provision towards the poor and unfortunate.

§ 17. *Were the Midianites made slaves? See Num.* 31 : 17–47

The treatment of the Midianites as recorded in Num. 31:

17–47, has been thought by some to involve enslavement.— The passage is too long to be quoted here. The reader will please refer to it.

The substance of it is this. While Israel sojourned in the desert, a portion of the people allowed themselves to be seduced by the Midianitish women to worship Baal Peor—the licentious Baal. God therefore sent a plague upon these miserable sinners in Israel, and cut off 24000 of them. (See Num. 25 : 9). In the 31st chapter, God enjoins upon Moses to execute vengeance upon the Midianites, for causing Israel to sin as they did against the Lord in the matter of Peor.— The Israelites armed themselves and went out against Midian. They slew all the males, and took the females and children captive. Finally Moses commanded that all these wicked women should be slain also, together with their male children. What now shall be done with the female children, and the spoils of sheep, beeves and asses? Moses commands that there shall be an equal division of all these between the soldiers and the people who, though willing to go out to the war, yet staid in the camp. The pro-slavery inference is, in regard to these thirty-two thousand captives, that inasmuch as they are mentioned as being divided in the same manner as the sheep and oxen, that therefore they were counted only as chattels. But this is a *non sequitur* altogether. The Lord's portion was thirty-two! Now what did the Lord want of thirty-two little female slaves? I can see how he wanted them to serve him in the service of the Tabernacle, and how, through the venerable priesthood of Aaron, they were taught and trained in the holy services of the Sanctuary—not as slaves, but as honored servants and handmaids of Jehovah.— Then three hundred and twenty of them fell to the Levites, not as slaves, but as servants in the priestly families of Israel, trained up in all the religious observances of the tribe of Levi, surrounded by every sacred moral influence in the Levitical households, sitting at the same table with the family— and in a word, accounted and treated with all the kindness of the children of the family—in all respects according to the

Hebrew law as above explained, and so it must have been done to the rest, divided to the other tribe.

§ 18. *Did Joshua enslave the Gibeonites?*

Mr. "X" is very sure that Joshua made slaves of the Gibeonites. The account is found in Joshua, 9: 22–27, and reads as follows: (I will present a literal version from the Hebrew.)

Verse 22. "And Joshua called unto them [the Gibeonites,] and spake unto them, saying, why have ye deceived us, saying, we [*live*] very far from you, but [*in fact*] ye dwell in the midst of us."

Verse 23. "And now ye are cursed. There shall not be one cut off from you [*but he shall be*] a servant, [i. e., every one of you shall be servants,] and ye shall be hewers of wood and drawers of water for the house of my God."

Verse 24. "And they answered Joshua and said, it was positively made known to thy servants, that Jehovah thy God strictly enjoined upon His servant Moses to give you all the land, and to destroy all the inhabitants of the land, and we feared greatly for our lives from before you, and we did this thing."

Verse 25. "And now behold we are in thy hand, according as is good and according as it is right in thine eyes to do to us, [*so*] do."

Verse 26. "And so he did unto them, and he delivered them out of the hand of the children of Israel, and they killed them not."

Verse 27. "And Joshua appointed them on that day to be hewers of wood and drawers of water for the congregation, and for the altar of Jehovah unto this day—at the place which he shall choose."

In this case it will be observed that there was no *enslaving* of these people, for the reason that they were voluntary servants. See v. 8, "And they said unto Joshua, we are thy servants." So, also, verse 11, "We are thy servants." They were not employed in the families of the Israelites at all, but resided in their own cities, tending their own flocks and herds, and exercised the functions of a distinct though not independent community. (See Josh. 10: 6–11.) Joshua saved them from their enemies, the Amorites. The injuries inflicted on them by Saul were avenged by the Almighty on his descendants. (See 2 Sam. 21: 1–9.) They served at the house of God, or the Tabernacle, and only a few of them comparatively, could have been engaged at any one time. The rest dwelt in their cities, one of which was a great city. The service they rendered was an honorable and pious service, and a natural tribute for the privilege of protection. No service seems to have been required of their wives and daughters.— On the return from the Babylonish captivity, they dwelt at Ophel, near the temple. (Neh. 3: 26.) They were called *Nethinim*, from the Hebrew root *Nathan*—to give, because they were given up, devoted to the service of God at the sanctuary. They were never bought or sold. They were therefore not slaves at all. (See Kitto's Cyclopedia, Art. *Slave*, from which the above remarks are condensed.) Observe, also, that they were appointed to this service at the Tabernacle, because they had *deceived* Joshua, and hence Joshua used the strong term "accursed." It is proper to view them, therefore, as criminals working out their sentence, and on this ground their service was not that of slaves. So this case of the Gibeonites utterly fails as an example of slavery.

§ 19. *Does Jer. 2: 14, imply Slavery ?*

The passage reads as follows, and is quoted by "X" as a pro-slavery text.

"Is Israel a servant? Is he a home-born *slave?*" It will be observed that our English version has put the word "slave" in italics, intimating thereby that there is no corresponding word in the original. This intimation is entirely correct.— There is no word for "slave" in the original. The passage literally rendered, runs thus: "Is Israel a servant? is he one born in the house? Why then is he a spoil?" i. e., one captured as spoil. The meaning is that Israel is not a servant,

but a son in the family of the Lord—born in honorable wed-
lock, and not merely born in the house, of dishonorable birth,
as *yalid bayith* usually means. It is hardly needful to add
that there is no proof of slavery here among the chosen people. It is only intimated that the condition of the servant is
ignoble in comparison with that of a son—and hence the
question, Is not Israel a son? Is he not honorably born, a
worthy member of the divine family? If so, then why is he
spoiled, why is he subjugated by the heathen Babylonians?—
The answer is implied in the previous verse—" He has hewn
out to himself broken cisterns which cannot hold water."

§ 20. *Does Is.* 14 : 12, *recognize Slavery?*

This passage is also referred to by " X " as recognizing slavery. It is lamentable to think that an intelligent man, an
educated man as I take Mr. " X " to be, should so far mistake the meaning of this beautiful passage of Isaiah as to refer it to such a wicked and accursed institution as American
slavery. Alas! what will become of the poor sheep, if they
have *such* shepherds to lead them into the green pastures of
the Divine Word. Here is a beautiful Messianic passage, and
he seems to see in it only the wicked and savage oppressions
of slavery! Allow me to present it in an English dress, imi-
tating as closely as possible the Hebrew original :—

1. For Jehovah shall have mercy upon Jacob,
     He will yet choose Israel,
     He will cause them to rest on their land,
     And the stranger shall be joined unto them,
     And they [the strangers] shall cleave unto the house of
       Jacob.
2. And the peoples shall take them and bring them to their
       place,
     And the house of Israel shall inherit them upon the land
       of Jehovah,
     For servants and for handmaidens they [the heathen]
       shall be,

And they [the Israelites] shall be captors of their captors,
And they shall rule over those [formerly] their oppressors.

We have in this passage an epitome of the blessed results
of the Gospel. Its influence shall be such as to break down
the wall of partition which separates the Jew from the Gentile, and unite them in loving embrace. The stranger shall
be joined unto Israel, and they [the strangers] shall cleave
unto the house of Jacob. And the poor Jews, scattered and
sifted among the nations, shall be taken by their Gentile brethren and be brought to their ancient home in Palestine. And
there the Gentiles, in thankfulness and love to the God of the
Hebrews, shall sit down with their brethren the Jews, and
wait at their feet as willing servants, and as captives by the
grace of the blessed Messiah, and thus the Jew shall rule over
those, through the power and grace of the Saviour, who were
formerly their oppressors. The loving spirit of our holy religion leads us to be willing servants of one another. Jesus
himself set the example when he washed the disciples' feet,
and so affectingly taught them as He had done, so they should
do for one another. And the further lesson of the Saviour
may be recalled, that they should be the greatest and chief
among the disciples who should be servant of all. This is
the kind of slavery to which I do not object. The more of it
the better!

That the Gentiles are to come in and serve the spiritual
Israel in this way is further evident from such parallel passages as Is. 60 : 10, and 49 : 23 :—

The sons of the stranger shall build thy walls,
Their kings shall minister unto thee.
Because in wrath I smote thee,
Then in my good pleasure I will have mercy upon thee.
And kings shall be thy nursing fathers,
And their queens thy nursing mothers,
They shall bow down to thee with their faces to the earth,
And they shall lick the dust of thy feet.

It is hardly necessary to remark that this strongly figurative language is not to be literally understood, as for example, the *licking the dust of Israel's feet;* but it implies a delighted and joyful yielding to the mild dominion of King Messiah, and a loving interest and regard for the ancient and chosen people. Precisely so are we to understand Is. 14 : 2.

And again allow me to remark how utterly abhorrent to the nice sense of justice, and the holy principle of love in the happy millennial period of the church, would be the *enslavement* of our brethren in Christ. How inconsistent their unwilling servitude, their work without wages, their subjection to arbitrary will, the frequent ruin of their dearest domestic ties which God himself has sanctified and saved from the ruins of the fall, and their debasing subjection to the condition of chattels and beasts of burden. I say how inconsistent would these things be in the happy reign of the Messiah, when the knowledge of the Lord shall cover the earth as the waters cover the sea. How inconsistent are they now in our day even! All these things and much more are involved in slavery. It is not a Christian institution. It was not even a Mosaic or Jewish institution. No Christian, after a proper study of the Scriptures and of the necessary character of slavery itself, can receive it as a divine institution.

§ 21. *Does Joel 3 : 6—8, imply enslavement?*

The passage reads as follows: "The children also of Judah and the children of Jerusalem, have ye sold unto the Grecians, that ye might remove them from their border. Behold I will raise them out of the place whither ye have sold them, and will return your recompense upon your own head; and I will sell your sons and your daughters into the hand of the children of Judah, and they shall sell them to the Sabeans, to a people far off, for the Lord hath spoken it."

These verses are a portion of Joel's prophecy against the heathen oppressors of the children of Israel. One of the horrid crimes of which these heathen became guilty, was the selling of the "children of Judah and the children of Jerusalem" into slavery to the Greeks. The anger of the Almighty was kindled against these heathen oppressors of his people, and he declares by his prophet Joel, that as they had sold Israel, he [Jehovah] would sell their sons and their daughters into the hand of the children of Judah, for their many and base crimes, and they should not keep them as slaves, but should sell them to the Sabeans—Arabians, to a people far off—as wicked criminals, whose presence could not be endured among the holy people—so defiled had they become with the beastly crimes mentioned in the third verse, as the sale of boys and girls for the purposes of prostitution, and for wine, that they might add to their other crimes that of drunkenness and general debauchery.

The face of the passage shows that there is no justified sale here of innocent persons. God condemned the Sidonians, Tyrians and Phœnicians for kidnapping and selling the Jews to the Greeks, and for these crimes he had these Sidonians sold to the Arabs for their punishment. This was justifiable, because for crime. This is the clearest case possible in vindication of my position. *All selling of human beings is condemned by it, except for crime.* As the thief was sold for his crime, till he by his labor had made ample restitution, so these Sidonians were sold by the Divine order, through Jewish merchants, to the fierce Sabeans or Arabians, to pay the penalty of *their* crimes by the loss of *their* personal liberty— it may have been during life. This very thing is done to criminals, in substance, by us, every day. We send such men to the State Prison for a term of years or for life. The State sets them at work, and takes the avails of their labor and appropriates them to its own purposes. And this is all right— and no slavery. The passage, therefore, does not suit slavery at all, and I am greatly surprised that " X " did not so see it.

§ 22. *Is Slavery directly and positively forbidden by the Old Testament?*

I think God's fundamental law is laid down in Exodus 21 : 16, (I render from the Hebrew,) *He that steals a man, or sells him, or if he be found in his hand, shall surely be put to death.*

This is the law of the old Testament. The law of the New Testament could go no further, nor do we desire that it should go any further. This law plainly makes *enslaving, selling, or holding a human being as a slave, each to be a capital crime.*

So the United States law says that the slave trade is piracy, and must be punished with death. So far we are up to the Jewish law. Now let me ask, if kidnapping be piracy; is not the holder of stolen goods exactly on a level with the thief? Is not slaveholding exactly on a level with slave stealing? Such is the statement of the Jewish law, and it is correct.

In accordance with this law was the subsequent preaching and teaching of the prophets Isaiah and Jeremiah: "Is not this the fast that I have chosen? to loose the bonds of wickedness, to undo the heavy burdens, and to let the oppressed go free, and that ye break every yoke?"—(Is. 58 : 6.) "Therefore thus saith the Lord, Ye have not hearkened unto me in proclaiming liberty, every one to his brother, and every man to his neighbor; behold I proclaim a liberty for you, saith the Lord, to the sword, to the pestilence, and to the famine."— (Jer. 34 : 17.)

And then the principle of wages for work, so emphatically declared both in the Law and the Prophets, is utterly at variance with the principle of slavery, which is always work without wages. See Deut. 24 : 14—"Thou shalt not oppress a hired servant, poor and needy of thy brethren or of thy strangers that are in thy land within thy gates. At his day thou shalt give his wages, neither shall the sun go down upon it, for he is poor and setteth his heart upon it, lest he cry against thee unto the Lord, and it be sin unto thee." See also Jeremiah 22 : 13—"Wo unto him   *   * that useth his neighbor's service without wages, and giveth him not for his work."

Now I would submit this simple question to my friend X.

Does the Old Testament contradict itself? Do the prophets teach a different doctrine from that contained in the Law? I think not. Consistency, therefore, as well as sound criticism, compel me to the belief that SLAVERY DID NOT EXIST AMONG THE CHOSEN PEOPLE, AND FURTHER, THAT IT IS POSITIVELY DIS- COUNTENANCED AND FORBIDDEN BOTH IN THE LAW AND IN THE PROPHETS.

§ 23. *What was the Jewish Servitude?*

The reader will naturally desire a condensed statement of what Jewish servitude was before we leave this part of our subject. I find the following condensed statement in Kitto's Cyclopedia, which is so conformatory of the views above ex- pressed, and so comprehensive and excellent that I prefer to give it to my readers rather than any thing I could myself prepare.

" Immediately after giving the law at Sinai, as if to guard against all slavery and slave trading on the part of the Israel- ites, God promulgated this ordinance, " he that stealeth a man and selleth him, or if he be found in his hands he shall surely be put to death. Ex. 21: 16, Deut. 24: 7. The crime is stated in its threefold form, *man stealing, selling* and *hold- ing.* The penalty for either of which was DEATH.

The law punished the stealing of mere property by enforc- ing restitution in some cases twofold in others fivefold, Ex. 22: 14, when property was stolen the legal penalty was com- pensation to the person injured; but when a man was stolen, no property compensation was allowed; DEATH was inflicted, and the guilty offender paid the forfeit of his life for his trans- gression ; God thereby declaring the infinite dignity and worth of man and the inviolability of his person. The reason of this may be found in the great fact, that God created man in his own image—Gen. 1: 26, 28.—a high distinction, more than once repeated with great solemnity—5: 1, 9: 6. Such was the operation of the law and the obedience paid to it, that we have not the remotest hint, that the sale and purchase of slaves, ever occurred among the Israilites. The cities of Judea were not like the cities of Greece and Rome, slave markets nor were there found throughout all its coasts either helots or slaves. With the Israelites service was either voluntary, or judicially imposed by the law of God,—Lev. 25: 39, 47, Ex. 21: 7, 22: 34, Deut. 20: 14.

The law gave Jewish servants many rights and privileges; they were admitted into covenant with God, Deut. 29: 10, 13. They were guests at all the national and family festivals Ex. 12: 43 44. Deut. 12: 18, 16: 10—16. They were statedly instructed in morals and religion Deut. 31: 10, 13. Josh. 8: 33, 2 Cor. 17: 8, 9, 25: 3, 34: 30, Neh. 8: 7, 8,— They were released from their regular labor nearly one half of their term of servitude, viz: every seventh year, Lev. 25: 3, 6, every seventh day Ex. 20: at the three annual festivals Ex. 23: 17, 34: 23, viz: the passover and feast of weeks, which lasted each seven days, and the feast of tabernacles which lasted eight. Also on the new moon the feast of trumpets and the day of atonement.

Besides these were the local festivals Judg. 21: 19, 1 Sam. 9: 12, 22, &c., and the various family feasts, as the weaning of children, marriages, sheep shearing, and circumcision the making of covenants 1 Sam. 20: 6, 28, 29. To these must be added the feast of Purim which lasted three days, and the dedication which lasted eight. The servants of the Israelites were protected by the law equally with their masters Deut. 1: 16, 17, 27: 19, Lev. 19: 15, 24: 22, Num. 15: 29—and their civil and religious rights were the same, Num. 15: 15, 16, 29. 9: 14, Deut. 1: 16, 17, Lev. 24: 22. To these might be added numerous passages which represent the Deity as regarding alike the natural rights of all, and making for all our equal provision 2 Ch. 19: 7, Prov. 24: 23, 28: 20, Job 34: 19, 2 Sam. 15: 14, Eph. 6: 9.

Finally these servants had the power of changing their masters and of seeking protection where they pleased, Deut. 23: 15, 16.

§ 24. *Did the Lord Jesus condemn Slavery?*

I think we may answer this question in the affirmative.

He did condemn it. He condemned it in his preaching in the synagogue at Nazareth, when he preached from the text, recorded in Is. 61 : 1, 2.

The account of this preaching in given in the fourth chapter of Luke commencing with the sixteenth verse. I will quote from the Greek.

"And he came unto Nazareth, where he was brought up ; and he entered in according to his custom on the Sabbath day into the synagogue, and stood up to read, and there was given to him the book of Isaiah the prophet, and having opened the book, he found the place where it was written. *" The spirit of the Lord is upon me, because he hath anointed me to preach the gospel to the poor ; he hath sent me to heal the broken in heart ; to preach freedom to the captives, and [to give] sight to the blind, liberty to the oppressed, and to herald forth the acceptable year of the Lord."*

"And having closed the book, and having given it to the attendant, he sat down; and the eyes of all in the synagogue were fixed upon him. He began to speak unto them, that this day this scripture [which I have just read,] is fulfilled in your ears, and all expressed approbation of him and wondered at the gracious words which came forth out of his mouth."

I think it must be conceded that preaching freedom to captives and liberty to the oppressed must have regard to the enslaved. If the Saviour did not preach an abolition sermon on this occasion from this scripture, his Sermon must have been very unlike his text.

But if there had been no Sermon, the text I think is sufficient to show that our Lord did indeed preach against slavery which is simply a system of oppression and bondage.

The supposed silence in respect to slavery of our Saviour is sought to be made a strong point by pro-slavery writers. Bishop Hopkins says "First then we ask what the divine Redeemer said in reference to slavery. And the answer is perfectly undeniable. HE DID NOT ALLUDE TO IT AT ALL. Not one word upon the subject is recorded by any of the four

Evangelists who gave his life and doctrines to the world, yet slavery was in full existence at the time throughout Judea; and the Roman Empire, according to Gibbon contained sixty millions of slaves, on the lowest probable computation."

The reader can say for himself whether the Saviour alluded to the subject of slavery at all in the Synagogue at Nazareth, and whether the prophet in the text has not a direct reference to slaveholding oppressions as well as others.

It is to be admitted however that specific references to the sin of slaveholding, were not to be expected in Judea, for the simple reason *that the institution of slavery was not there.* It was indeed among the Greeks and Romans, but neither of these nations imposed their peculiar institutions upon their conquered provinces. After their subjection to the Romans the Jews still continued to live under the laws and institutions of the Old Testament. They paid tribute to Cæsar, and were under a Roman Governor, but there is no evidence that Roman institutions as idolatry and slavery were ever imposed upon them.

This to my mind is a sufficient reason why we do not have more specific references to the sin of slavery by our Lord and the apostles. Indeed we have all that under the circumstances we could expect

§ 25. *Does our Saviour "allude" to Slavery in Mark* 10: 41–44 ?

With all *due* deference to Bishop Hopkins I think he does. Let us read the passage.

"*And the ten* [i. e. the other ten apostles] *having heard* [the ambitious request mentioned in the previous verses] *began to be displeased concerning James and John. But Jesus having called them says to them, Ye know that those who rule over the Gentiles exercise lordship over them, and their great ones exercise authority over them;* [as masters over their slaves,] *but it shall not be so among you* [my disciples,] *but whosoever would be great among you let him be your deacon, and whosoever would be first among you shall be* DOULOS *of all.*

I think there must be an allusion here to the slave power as it existed in our Saviour's day among the Gentiles. If the slave power existed in all its perfection among the chosen people as Bishop Hopkins contends, then why should the Saviour go to the Gentiles for an example which was occurring every day before his eyes. However this may be the passage is a most crushing condemnation of the whole spirit and practice of slavery in the church of God. "IT SHALL NOT BE SO AMONG YOU!" *Precious, divine words!*

The great principles contained in the Saviour's words, *"thou shalt love thy neighbor as thyself,"* and in *"whatsoever ye would that men should do to you, do ye even so to them,"* at once destroys the whole system of slavery,—in such a divine atmosphere it withers and dies away. What has become of the sixty millions of slaves of the Roman Empire? There can be but one answer to this question, the Bible has under God emancipated them! Behold this triumph! Why should Dr. Lord and Bishop Hopkins wish it otherwise? And why should they seek to stay this divine power in its onward progress of emancipation in our own land? They cannot do it. The decree of God has gone forth!

§ 26. *Did the Apostles condemn Slavery?*

Art thou called being a servant, care not for it, but if thou art able to be free use it rather. 1 Cor. 7: 21. The apostle probably alludes to involuntary servitude. If so the condition is condemned in the counsel to accept of freedom if it may be had. In other words be free rather than a slave if it be in your power.

Further the tender exhortation of the apostle " to remember those that are in bonds as bound with them " indicates his solicitude for those who were in the unfortunate condition of slavery. And therefore the institution is by these words condemned. Heb. 13: 3.

Again the apostle to Timothy, 1 Tim. 1: 8, 9, 10, says: " *The law was made not for a righteous man,* * * * *but for men* stealers, *for liars, for perjured persons,*"—for *men stealers* or *slave dealers.* *Slave dealers* are here condemned by the apostle, along with *liars* and *perjured persons.* But if God approves of slavery, then why should the apostle condemn those in the worthy employment of slave trading? There can be but one answer to this question. The apostle condemns the slavetrader because his business is wrong, and by consequence the institution of slavery which requires such a business.

St. John also sets his seal of reprobation upon this "sum of all villanies" when he reckons the "*merchandize in the bodies and souls of men*" as among the sins of Babylon the mother of Harlots. Rev. 18: 13.

No argument can be drawn in favor of slavery from the fact that the apostle Paul lays down the reciprocal duties of masters and servants, whether voluntary or involuntary. The passage of this class most commonly referred to and supposed to sanction slavery, is 1 Tim. 6: 1, 2.

"Let as many as are servants under the yoke, count their own masters worthy of all honor, that the name and doctrine of God be not blasphemed. Let those having believing masters not despise them, because they are brethren, but rather let them serve, because they are faithful and beloved—partakers of the good cause."

In this passage two classes of masters are referred to—1, "*masters,*" 2, "*believing masters*"—but whether they were *slave* masters or merely *servant* masters is not clear. Probably both are meant by the apostles. Nor can anything be inferred from the phrase "servants under the yoke," whether slave servants are meant or ordinary servants for wages.— Our Saviour said, "take my yoke upon you," "my yoke is easy," i. e., my service is easy. It is not thereby implied that Christians are Christ's slaves! Nor is it necessary to understand the apostolic injunction here of persons in slavery exclusively. I grant that the injunction *may* refer to such; it refers, also, just as much to ordinary servants, those who serve for wages. I think it embraces both classes, and not either exclusively. But this admission cannot be construed as a

justification of the cruel system of slavery, by any means—
only that heathen masters are to be properly respected and
obeyed. So likewise "believing masters"—Christian masters
are not to be despised, "because they are brethren."

However it may have been with heathen masters, it could
not have been with Christian masters that they were slaveholders, or slave drivers, or slave sellers, for the relation of
"*brethren*," "faithful and beloved," would preclude all such
ideas. The moment a man becomes a Christian, that moment
all whips, all manacles, all chains, all withholdment of wages,
cease,—and the phrase "Christian slaveholder," is a contradic-
tion in terms. The command to masters to render unto their
servants that which is just and equal, (Col. 4: 1,) supposing
them to be slave masters, utterly subverts the relation of slavery; for slavery in its essence is *injustice* and *inequality*.

§ 27. *Did Paul send back Onesimus to Philemon as a fugitive slave?*

By no means, *as a slave.* For Paul expressly says, verse
16, *Not now as a servant, but above a servant, a brother beloved.*
Nor is it certain that he ever was a *slave* to Philemon or any
other man. He was or had been a servant—a *doulos*—but
there is no evidence that he had been a slave. He being in
debt to Philemon had left him. In what way the debt was
contracted does not appear. Paul says if he hath wronged
thee or oweth thee aught, put that on mine account. I, Paul,
have written it with my own hand. *I will repay it.* There is
no other evidence in the text that Onesimus was a slave except what is derived from the use of the term *doulos*, but this
does not imply that he was a slave any more than that the
apostle Paul was a slave, for he calls himself a *doulos* of Jesus Christ.

§ 28. *The Old Testament and the New in harmony against
Slavery.*

The Scriptures are a unit in their testimony against slavery. If the view presented in the previous pages be correct, Bishop Hopkins will not find fault with it because it puts one portion of Holy Scripture in antagonism with another. Nor will Mr. X. inquire of me what part of the *Old Testament* is *repealed* on the subject of slavery. I hold that the Old Testament is God's word as well as the New. Our Saviour and the apostles honored the Old Testament. It was their Bible. It is that Series of Sacred books which *Holy men of old wrote as they were moved by the Holy Ghost.* Our Saviour came *not to destroy the law and the prophecy but to fulfill them*," and no part or parts of these sacred books are repealed except what is definitely declared to be so repealed by the Divine and inspired authority of Christ himself and the Holy Apostles.

CONTENTS.

www.ingramcontent.com/pod-product-compliance
Lightning Source LLC
Chambersburg PA
CBHW022024080426
42733CB00007B/719